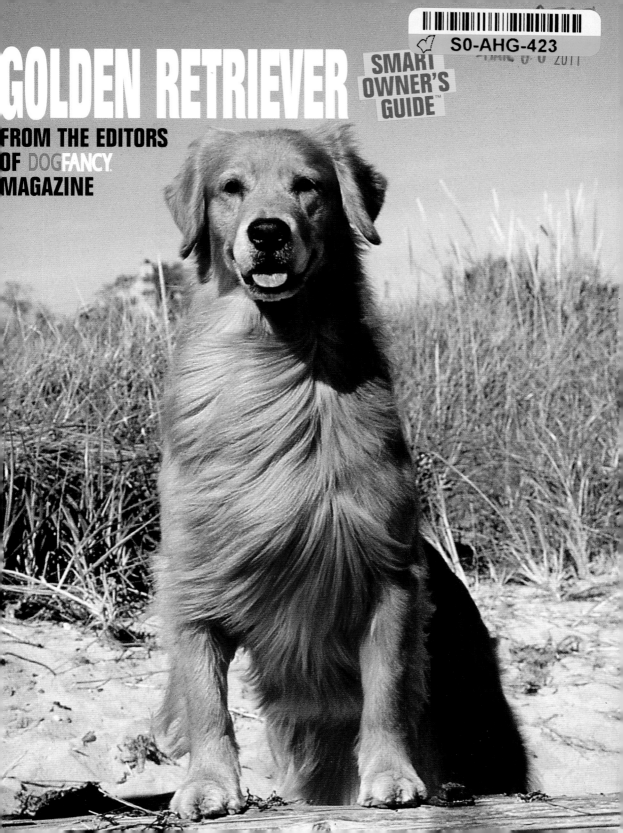

GOLDEN RETRIEVER

SMART OWNER'S GUIDE™

FROM THE EDITORS OF DOGFANCY MAGAZINE

CONTENTS

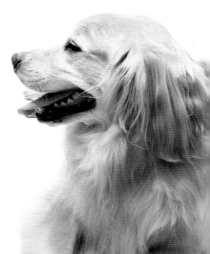
Golden Retriever, a Smart Owner's Guide™
part of the Kennel Club Books® Interactive Series™
ISBN: 978-1-593787-76-9. ©2009

Kennel Club Books Inc., 40 Broad St., Freehold, NJ 07728. Printed in China.
All rights reserved. No part of this book may be reproduced in any form,
by Photostat, scanner, microfilm, xerography or any other means, or incorporated
into any information retrieval system, electronic or mechanical,
without the written permission of the copyright owner.

*photographers include Isabelle Francias/BowTie Inc.; Tara Darling/BowTie Inc.; Gina
Cioli and Pamela Hunnicutt/BowTie Inc. Contributing writer: Nona Kilgore Bauer*

For CIP information, see page 176.

K9 EXPERT

Welcome to the wonderful world of Goldens! It's no accident that they're called Golden Retrievers, you know.

Of course, their gorgeous coats are rich and lustrous, whether they're on the pale side or on the reddish end of gold. There's no mistaking a Golden. That coat gives them away immediately.

What comes with striking beauty, though, is big grooming responsibility. Most Goldens need daily brushing. Fortunately, this is a task you can turn over to a child — most of the time. You'll still need to brush at least weekly to do the longer hair — on the legs, around the neck and ears, under the body and on that graceful tail feathering.

But brushing shouldn't be a chore. It's a time for your children and you to connect with your dog, further building the bond you already share. And it offers a great opportunity to find little bumps that could grow into something more sinister if ignored.

Now on to the retriever part. It means just what it sounds like. Your dog wants — no needs — to retrieve. Whether you throw a ball in the yard or a disc at the park, he requires this activity — and thrives on it.

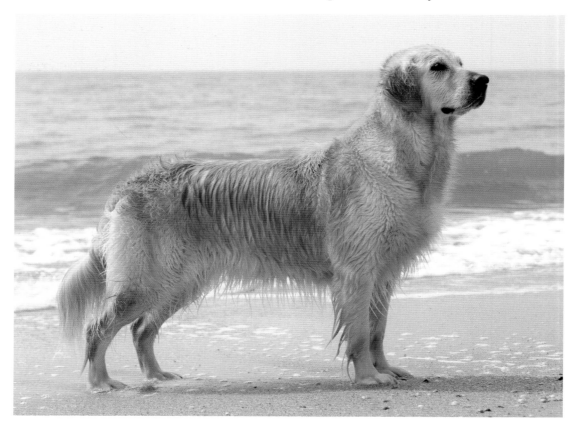

Don't be surprised if he likes to carry a stuffed animal around in his mouth. That's what Goldens' jobs were as hunting dogs. The urge to retrieve is still in them — even if they live the city, with no wild game around.

You certainly know this breed's reputation as the quintessential family dog. It's very likely why you're considering, or have already decided on, a Golden. However, you should know that these dogs aren't born perfect. Your Golden will be a very busy dog for at least the first 18 months.

So, you need to get an immediate start on socializing and training your new pal, and giving him plenty of exercise. That three-pronged effort will turn your rambunctious puppy and even busier adolescent into an amazing adult dog.

He'll be friendly right away. That's not a problem. He'll play with anyone who knows what a tennis ball is really for or who will pay him a little attention.

But he won't know how to sit or come or keep out of your kitchen wastebasket. He will entertain himself by chewing, digging and barking if he doesn't learn his manners and get enough exercise.

If you teach him what's OK and what's not, and instill a willing, reliable response to your cues, your Golden will become a model canine citizen.

It will take a couple of good walks each day — and at least one long session of fetch — to keep him well exercised. If you love to jog or swim, you'll find a ready partner once his bones are fully developed and he's acclimated to water.

As they say, a tired Golden is a happy Golden. And a happy Golden Retriever

With this Smart Owner's Guide™, you are well on your way to getting your Golden diploma. But your Golden Retriever education doesn't end here.

You're invited to join in **Club Gold™** (**DogChannel.com/Club-Gold**), a FREE online site with lots of fun and instructive features such as:

◆ **forums, blogs** and **profiles** where you can connect with other Golden Retriever owners
◆ **downloadable charts** and **checklists** to help you be a smart and loving Golden owner
◆ access to Golden Retriever **e-cards** and **wallpapers**
◆ interactive **games**
◆ canine **quizzes**

The **Smart Owner's Guide** series and **Club Gold** are backed by the experts at DOG FANCY® magazine and DogChannel.com — who have been providing trusted and up-to-date information about dogs and dog people for more than 40 years. Log on and join the club today!

JOIN OUR ONLINE Club Gold™

makes for a very happy Golden Retriever owner. Soon, you'll have the kind of family dog that everyone wants: loving, friendly and well behaved. Enjoy!

Susan Chaney
Editor, DOG FANCY

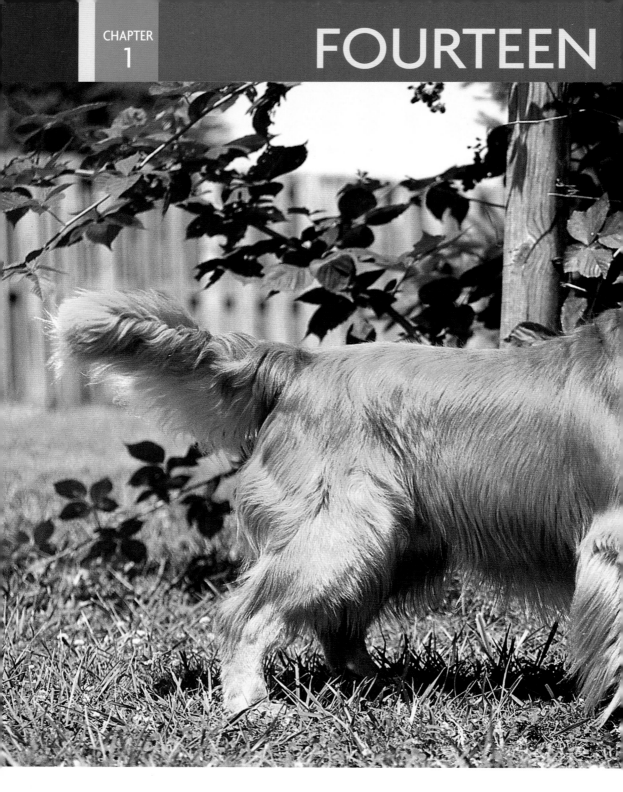

KARAT

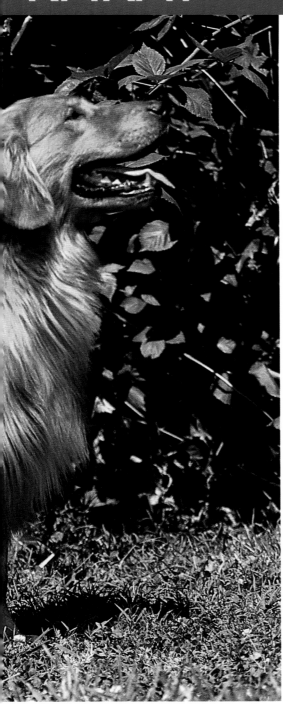

Gentle, kind and affectionate: The breed of dog that most often comes to mind at the sound of these adjectives is the Golden Retriever.

The Golden comes by this reputation with good reason. Of all the hundreds of dog breeds in the world, the Golden Retriever is one of the sweetest, most giving canines on earth. Goldens work as therapy dogs, service dogs and search-and-rescue dogs, and they provide loyalty and companionship to children and adults alike. And, as most people know, Golden Retrievers have a smile and a wagging tail for just about everyone they meet.

Of course, it's no accident that Goldens are such wonderful dogs. Breeders have worked hard over the decades to develop and preserve this wonderful temperament.

In fact, the American Kennel Club Golden Retriever breed standard (a written description of what an ideal Golden should look and act like) has a section devoted exclusively

> **it's a Fact**
>
> **Thievery is common among Golden Retrievers,** but unlike other breeds, these dogs are doing it mostly because of the retrieving instinct rather than out of sneakiness. When they're not stealing your household items, Goldens will find other objects to carry; sometimes when they can't figure out what to carry, they try to carry as much as they can.

to temperament. The section describes the breed as "friendly, reliable and trustworthy." These qualities — and more — are what breeders of Golden Retrievers strive for today.

"Golden Retrievers have a pleasing nature and are very intelligent and trainable," says breeder Amanda L. Dorner of Hyline Kennels in Palmyra, Wisc. "They actually smile by curling up the corners of their mouths and showing some teeth. Often, they are comical and entertaining, and they make up games. They are also very intuitive and sense many things. I truly believe they understand what you say to them. They try very hard to communicate with their owners, and the closer the bond, the more successful they are. They are also very observant and notice the strangest things."

According to breeder Melissa Johnston of Clarkcreek Golden Retrievers in Clark, Penn., a Golden with an ideal temperament is one that is a willing worker, eager to please, lives to be with his people and has the think-it-through mentality of many great sporting dogs.

"He also has to possess the drive and athletic ability to hunt, play and fulfill the sporting dog role he was bred for," Johnston says. "By and large, most Goldens are unflappable. They love people, kids and other animals, and will gladly run through fire if that is what you ask of them."

The Golden Retriever is known for being a benevolent and softhearted dog; however, Johnston cautions against unrealistic expectations of the breed. "I disagree with the image of a Golden as a large, plush, sugary-sweet, syrupy kind of dog that never shows any signs of being a dog," Johnston says. "By this, I mean I do not believe a dog – any dog

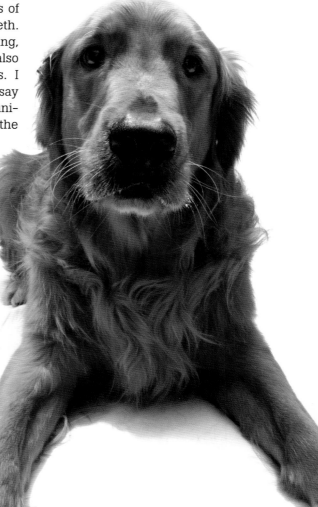

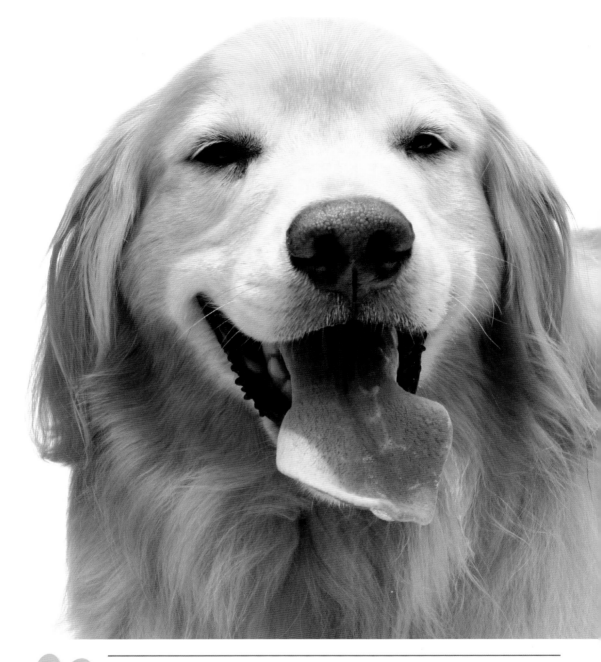

Meet other Golden owners just like you. On our Golden forums, you can chat about your Golden Retriever and ask other owners for advice on training, health issues and anything else about your favorite dog breed. Log onto **DogChannel.com/Club-Gold** for details!

— is supposed to be a big blob willing to endure endless hours of torment from another dog, child and so on."

However, despite this truth, the Golden is considered one of the most tolerant dog breeds around. A trait which makes the breed uniquely suited to being an excellent companion while fulfilling some of the most challenging canine jobs around.

PERFECT PETS

The Golden Retriever's distinctive temperament makes the breed incredibly popular as a friend and companion, and it's easy to see why. Golden Retriever owners have a myriad of stories to tell about the wonders of living with a Golden.

"Goldens have a keen sense of smell and are determined to follow through to the end of a task that they believe will please their owner," Dorner says. "For example, if our Goldens were out, our family could never clear our yard of sticks, fallen apples and other debris by tossing it in the woods — as the dogs would retrieve it all. They would just look and look until they found just the item that you threw. In fact, I once looked closely at a fallen apple for identifying marks before I tossed it in the woods. I threw it deep. It took some time, but one of my Goldens returned the exact apple to me."

Goldens are just as tenacious about hunting. "Goldens love to hunt and do it quite naturally," Dorner says. "One time, my dog April brought me a huge opossum that

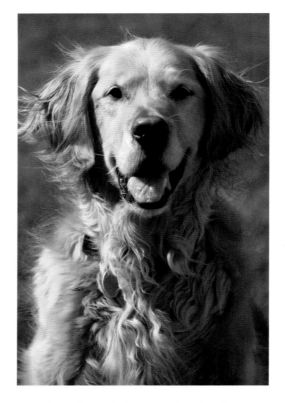

must have been in its den sleeping because it was daytime. The opossum was so big, April could barely carry it, but carry it she did, with the opossum snarling and hissing. I had my other dogs loose in the yard at the time, so it was difficult to deflect their excitement about April's great find and get them all put away so the opossum could go back where it came from!"

Linda Giorgi has also lived with great Golden hunters, including one dog named Bo, whose intense retrieving instinct once got him into trouble. "Bo was up for anything,

---

Show your artistic side. Share photos, videos and artwork of your favorite breed on Club Gold. You can also submit jokes, riddles and even poetry about Golden Retrievers. Browse through our various galleries and see the talent of fellow Golden owners. Go to **DogChannel.com/Club-Gold** and click on "Galleries" to get started.

JOIN OUR ONLINE Club Gold™

had great courage in the field and had an uncanny ability to open any door or kennel," Giorgi says. "His insatiable curiosity got him into some problems in his life. He would fetch and deliver anything shot. On one occasion, a skunk was shot, and while trying to return the 'catch' to his panicked owner, Bo kept on coming with eyes tearing and his mouth foaming from the foul taste. He was determined to get that game back to his handler, who was running in the opposite direction at the time. Bo simply increased his pace to catch his now-sprinting owner."

Another distinctive facet of the Golden's temperament is his versatility. Goldens can work hard in the field one hour and be a child's perfect companion the next. Johnston tells of one of her female Goldens named Winter, who absolutely adores being around kids. "Winter is a wild child and full of as much energy as any dog I have ever owned, except when in the company of children," Johnston says. "Then, she is calm, makes deliberate and slow

movements and is never, ever even close to the activity level she resumes when in the company of adult family and friends. I have no idea why, except that maybe it's her sixth doggie sense. She loves everyone and will pester you until you acknowledge she is the best dog alive. Maybe with children it is an unwritten rule; they know she is the best dog alive and are willing to show it the minute they meet her."

A SIXTH SENSE

The Golden Retriever is friendly and forgiving, making him popular among those who provide pet-assisted therapy to patients in nursing homes, hospitals and other institutions. "For therapy work in particular, I don't know of a better breed," Johnston says. "Golden Retrievers seem to possess a sixth sense about when someone

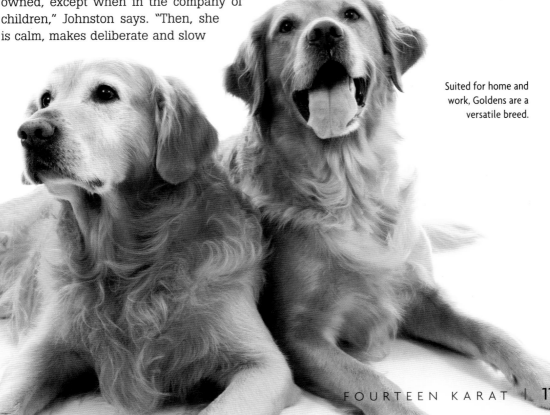

Suited for home and work, Goldens are a versatile breed.

is in distress, needs help or just needs comforting. Many of our Goldens have become Therapy Dog International dogs used in hospitals around the country. Because Goldens have a natural love of people, many of them seem to thrive in this environment."

One example of that special Golden Retriever sixth sense is evident in Lana, owned by Helena Weil, a clinical psychologist and director of a pain center in Castro Valley, Calif. "Lana has been working with me at the pain center four days a week," Weil says. "She has this amazing ability to sense people's pain. I have never before met a dog with this uncanny ability to connect to people."

Lana, who earned her AKC championship under the guidance of her breeder — Ann Chase of Honor Golden Retrievers in Mineral Springs, N.C., is invaluable in Weil's practice. "When I counsel people, they tell me they feel better because Lana is in the room with them," she says. "Petting Lana seems to stimulate the production of endorphins that block pain in these patients."

Lana seems to understand her job at the pain center and works to help patients interact with her as much as they can. "I have one patient, a woman in her late 70s," Weil says. "She's on very heavy pain medication, yet the pain still doesn't go away. She has problems with her feet and legs and uses a walker to get around. Every time this woman walks into my office, Lana positions herself so the woman can pet her without straining. This patient didn't feel comfortable talking to anyone at first, but then she started talking to Lana."

Another part of Lana's job is to travel around the center with Weil, visiting patients and encouraging them in their attempts to overcome their pain. "We go to the pool

where people are swimming, and she goes right up to the edge so people can pet her," Weil says. "We go to the rehabilitation area where the physical therapists are working. We even go to the surgery center. Of course, Lana doesn't only stick by the patients; she greets everyone. But with the patients, she has a specific way of greeting them: by lying by their feet and letting them show her what they need. She is very gentle with all of them." According to Weil, Lana has made such an impression at her job that other psychologist want to get dogs like her and integrate them into hospital settings.

Another amazing Golden Retriever working hard at pet-assisted therapy is Cedar, owned by Carl Liepmann, a retired firefighter in Flushing, Mich. Cedar volunteers once a week at a closed-head-injury facility, where he helps patients overcome brain trauma. "Cedar is an excellent therapy dog," Liepmann says. "He has learned to be around people with head injuries, which can be challenging for a dog. People with this kind of injury have little control over their arms, and they will want to pet him

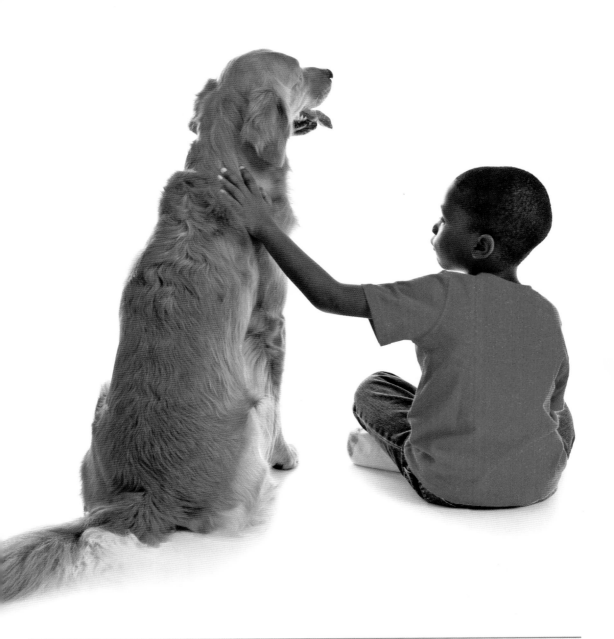

One of my Goldens constantly has two things in his mouth — two balls; a ball and a woobie [a beloved dog toy]; two woobies; a ball and a shoe; a woobie and a shoe; or two shoes. He doesn't tear them up; he just carries them around with him.

— *Kay Hepker of Center Point, Iowa*

but will sometimes smack him on top of the head instead. Cedar doesn't mind it, though, he is extremely tolerant."

That famous Golden Retriever sixth sense is apparent in Cedar. "One fellow we see at the facility will suddenly scream for no apparent reason," Liepmann says. "It used to scare me to death, but it never upset Cedar. I couldn't figure out why until I noticed that Cedar starts to wag his tail just before the patient is going to scream. Cedar knows the patient is about to do this and is prepared. And now when I see Cedar wagging his tail, I know it's coming."

Cedar has another job that only comes once a year: playing Santa Dog to support Liepmann's local humane society. "Cedar gets dressed up like Santa at Christmas time, and kids come and take pictures with him," Liepmann says. "He sits calmly on the table for nine to 10 hours a day with everyone petting him. He's amazing."

As evidence of the Golden Retriever's versatility, Liepmann points out that Cedar does a lot more than play Santa and provide pet-assisted therapy to patients at the trauma center. "He's a champion and an excellent hunting dog on waterfowl and upland game," Liepmann says. "We are also working on getting him obedience titles."

it's a **Fact**

You might love the Golden's glittering personality, but as with most great things, there's a downside. In this case, it's the shedding. Goldens shed consistently and they "blow" their coat (shed lots of fur all at once) about twice a year.

DRAWN TOWARD PEOPLE

Because Golden Retrievers are so people-oriented, they make excellent candidates for search-and-rescue dogs. SAR dogs are trained to locate lost people and victims of disasters, and are usually volunteers, as are their handlers.

Taylor is one such dog. A 7-year-old female Golden trained by her owner, Cheryl Gorewitz of Redding, Calif., Taylor started her basic training when she was only 7 weeks old. "By the age of 13 months, Taylor was certified as a search-ready, trailing SAR K9 for the Shasta County Sheriff's SAR Dog Team," Gorewitz says.

Taylor proved her worth as a SAR dog in when an inmate escaped from the Shasta County Jail. "After law enforcement personnel secured a perimeter around the area where the escapee was last seen, Taylor and I were called upon to attempt to locate the felon," Gorewitz says. "Without benefit of a scent article, and no confirmed track, Taylor and I set out, accompanied by two armed officers.

"Utilizing trailing and air-scenting skills, Taylor initially tracked, then air scented the subject, who had secreted himself in a grove of cedar trees and brush, laying face down on the ground in an attempt to avoid detection. Unfortunately for him, the nose knows! In less than 10 minutes from the start of the trail, the escapee was once again in custody and secured in the back of a patrol vehicle."

Tonka is a Golden Retriever currently studying to become a certified SAR dog like Taylor. Owned by Craig Pitcher of Dixon, Calif., Tonka is only 20 months old but is already showing considerable talent as a SAR dog. "Tonka loves to play and is eager to please, and these two traits make him easy to train for search-and-rescue," Pitcher says.

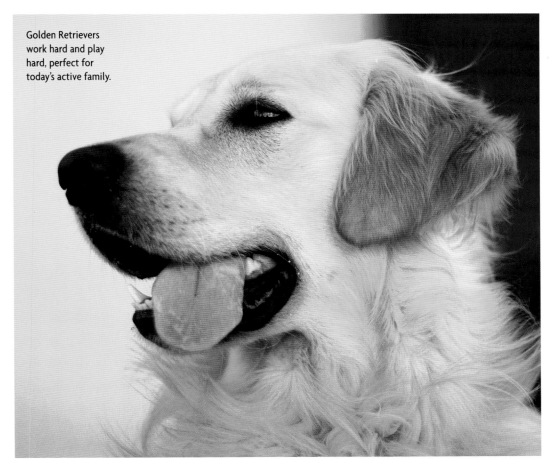

Golden Retrievers work hard and play hard, perfect for today's active family.

Tonka is currently learning to use air scenting to find any human in his general vicinity and will work at wilderness searches with volunteer groups in Northern California once he receives his certification. "I eventually hope to get into doing urban searching and disaster work," Pitcher says. "Right now, though, we are learning to work as a team and communicate with each other."

Unlike volunteers Gorewitz and Taylor and Pitcher and Tonka, some Golden Retriever SAR dogs are professionals. One such working dog is Riley, owned by a Federal Bureau of Investigation special agent in Washington, D.C., who prefers to be referred to only as Eileen. Riley came to Eileen as a puppy with the idea of turning the dog into an FBI SAR canine.

Riley started in obedience classes where she showed her worth as a potential SAR dog immediately. She was then certified as an official FBI SAR dog, and her job was to work at disaster sites to locate victims and also to track down criminals who were fleeing from the FBI. The Golden Retriever's attraction to people makes him particularly valuable as a search-and-rescue dog, to lost people's joy and criminals' chagrin.

HAPPY TO SERVE

Golden Retrievers can do more than just provide companionship to the convalescing and search for the missing. They also make skilled assistants for the handicapped in the form of service dogs.

Carol Bowes of Tequesta, Fla., raises puppies for Canine Companions International, a California-based organization that breeds and trains dogs as mobility and hearing assistants. She says that Goldens are ideally suited to be service dogs, whether for the sight, hearing or mobility impaired, and excel as service dogs for many of the same reasons they do well as therapy dogs. "Most Goldens are sensitive and get upset if you are displeased with them," Bowes says. "You don't have to yell at them. They live to please you."

Kevin Korobko of Cary, N.C., lives with a Golden service dog named Shamu. Korobko is wheelchair-bound. "Shamu is so eager to please," Korobko says. "He gets so excited when I ask for anything. His tail goes crazy, and he's very affectionate."

When David Gordon of Lindon, Utah, first applied for a guide dog, he didn't think he wanted a longhaired dog, such as a Golden. However, Gordon, who is sight-impaired, knew that Guide Dogs for the Blind in San Rafael, Calif., looks for the best match between dog and owner regardless of breed.

"I'd had five back surgeries, and I needed a dog that didn't pull hard," Gordon remembers. "That dog was Severin."

Gordon and Severin worked together for four years until Severin developed brain cancer at the age of 6. Gordon knew he

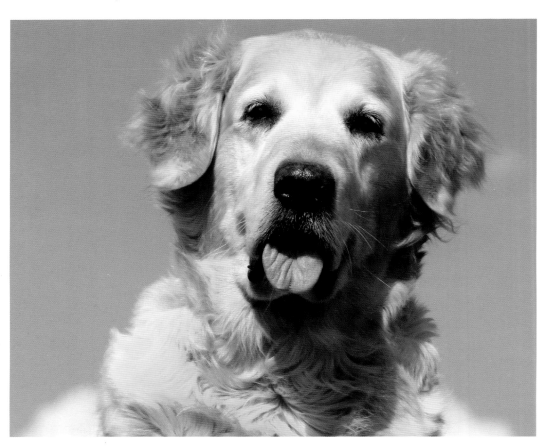

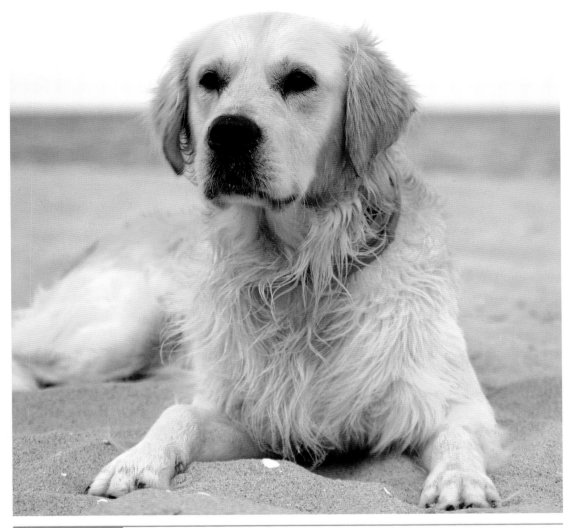

Golden people say that we brush an entire Pomeranian out of our dogs; that's how much dog hair we can get when we brush them. Immediately after I'm done vacuuming or sweeping the floors, there are little golden tumbleweeds floating around. Golden people also say that dog hair is a condiment; we are constantly picking it out of our food and out of our mouths! It's everywhere. I scoop out large golden dust bunnies from the bottom of the pool every day.

— Golden owner Tami Roleff of Yucca Valley, Calif.

would eventually need another service dog, and soon Harding, another Golden, joined the family.

Gordon recalls the day Severin "stepped down" and turned over his duties. "Severin knew when it was his time to give up the reins to Harding," he says. "We were all going to a doctor's appointment, and when we arrived, I picked up the harnesses. Instead of jumping up like he usually does, Severin just turned and looked at Harding. He never even stood up. It was a cool day, so I left him in the van. From then on, Harding was in charge."

Despite his initial reluctance to get a dog with a long coat, Gordon is now committed to Golden Retrievers. "Goldens have a gentleness and a very, very strong desire to please," he says. "When you praise them, their tails go 100 miles per hour. They're just as proud as punch. They really bond quickly with people, especially if they can tell you really care about them."

Before Severin, Gordon had navigated with a cane. Now that he's been guided by Golden Retrievers, however, he'll never go back. "I felt confident with the cane, but I'm even more confident with my Golden," he says. "In dangerous situations, a service dog can keep you out of trouble. Now, I'll even go on the New York City subway system to visit my daughter."

With a temperament designed for hunting, retrieving, helping humans and just being an overall great companion, it's no wonder the Golden Retriever has the reputation he does for being such a wonderful dog. "For me, there are no negative temperament issues with Goldens," Dorner says. "They are very true to their retrieving instinct and have a sense of humor. And they love to help and entertain."

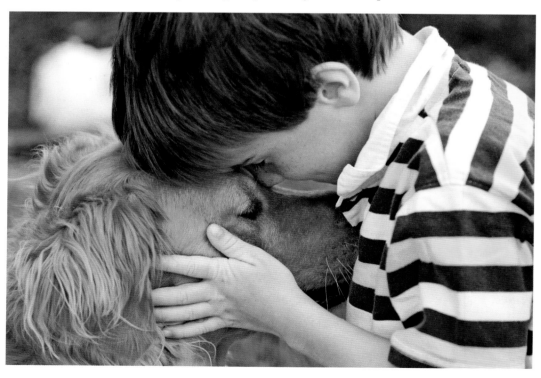

Addicted to Helping

Erin Renzelli and Nick met online. She had been searching the Internet, looking for just the right match — a canine partner. With his blond good looks and outgoing personality, Nick filled the bill.

"Nick's kind of special to me because it took me forever to find him," Renzelli says. "I searched and searched and searched and finally ran across him on the Internet."

At first glance, Nick's background might have made him seem like a dubious choice for a partner. He'd been evicted from several homes for unbecoming behavior. At Keystone Golden Retriever Rescue in Pennsylvania, they despaired of finding the right place for him. Then Renzelli came calling. Nick's exuberance and energy were just what she was looking for — in a drug detection dog.

Cpl. Renzelli is employed by Pruntytown Correctional Center in Grafton, W.V. She and Nick check inmates and visitors to make sure they're not bringing in drugs. In their spare time, they assist law enforcement officials by searching schools for drugs.

Nick, who was called "Snoopy" in his previous life, is named for one of Renzelli's fellow officers, who died at age 26. "That makes him even more important to me," she says.

Their job is in the way of being a preventive measure, so Nick doesn't have any major drug busts to his credit. That's OK. He still gets plenty of chances to show how good he is during regular training sessions.

"We train every week, and every six months we have to go through recertification," Renzelli says. "He loves finding drugs. He just has that desire, which makes him a good dog."

Nick indicates a find by sitting. If the drugs are within reach, he places his nose on them. Otherwise, he just sits as close to the odor as he can.

It looks as if Nick has finally found a lasting home. "I've had Labrador Retrievers all my life," Renzelli says, "but I'll tell you now that after having a Golden Retriever, I don't think I could have another breed. He's so smart and lovable."

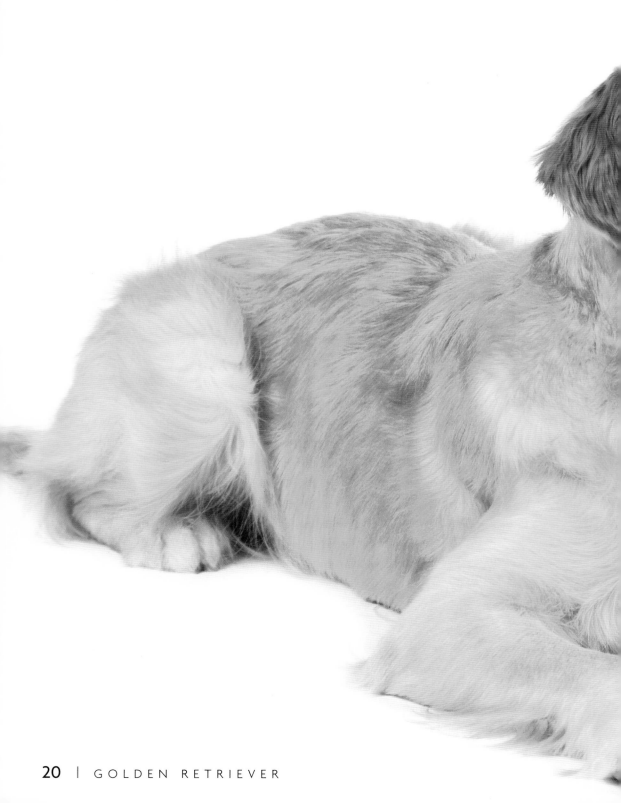

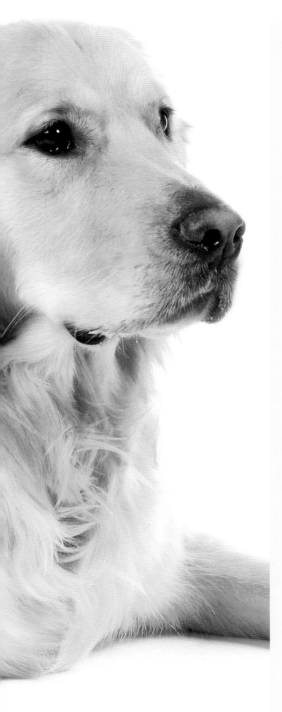

THE RETRIEVER REPORT

Lovable and loyal, these dogs are the perfect family companions.

COUNTRY OF ORIGIN: Great Britain/Scotland

WHAT HIS FRIENDS CALL HIM: Goldie, Goldilocks, Midas, Knox

SIZE: 22.5 to 24 inches tall; 55 to 75 pounds

COAT & COLOR: The Golden Retriever has a medium length coat with a dense undercoat and water-repellent outer coat. The coat can come in many shades of gold and can be wavy or straight.

PERSONALITY TRAITS: Goldens are outgoing, friendly, playful and even tempered; they get along with pretty much everyone.

WITH KIDS: These friendly dogs are great with children of all ages.

WITH OTHER PETS: good

ENERGY LEVEL: moderate to high

EXERCISE NEEDS: Exercise is key to keeping this dog happy, healthy and out of trouble.

GROOMING NEEDS: low maintenance, but sheds heavily two times a year

TRAINING NEEDS: These dogs are very easily trained. They excel in obedience work, as a guide dog and in activities such as hunting, search and rescue, and assistance work.

LIVING ENVIRONMENT: Golden Retrievers do best with a yard in a rural or suburban area.

LIFESPAN: 10 to 12 years

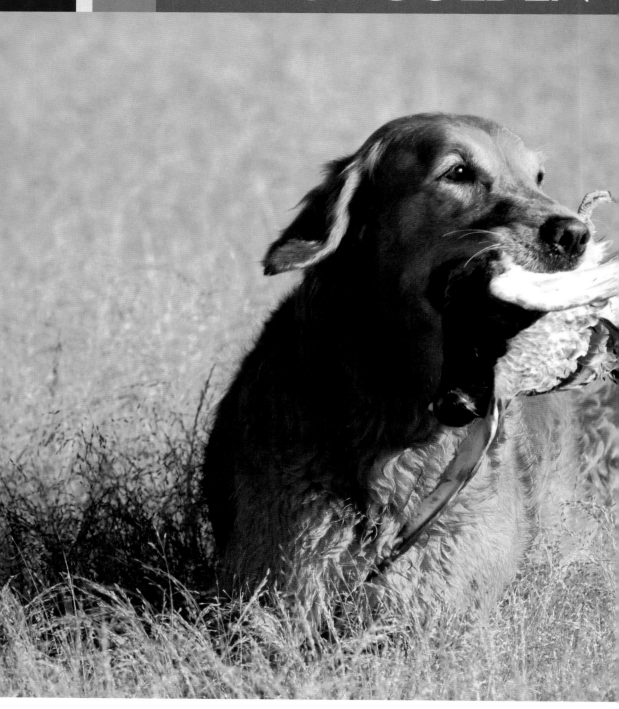

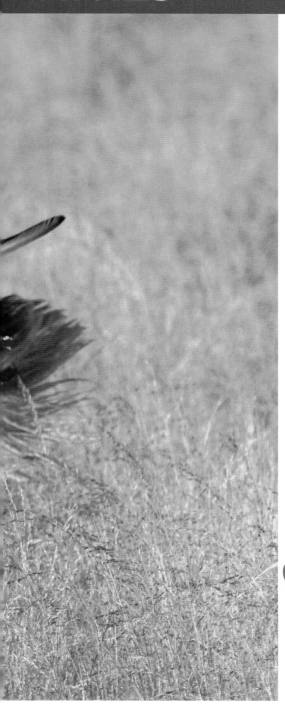

They're everywhere! It's no surprise to see at least one Golden Retriever in every neighborhood. They're still the favorite canine face on everything from dog food packaging to TV commercials and catalog ads. They're also a joy for groomers, veterinarians and other dog professionals. How could you not love them, with those happy smiles and huge brown eyes that beg for a squeeze?

Those who live with Goldens nod knowingly. Once you own a Golden, you become a raving lunatic about the breed. Doesn't every Golden family claim their dog is actually one of their children dressed in a golden fur coat? Dog stuff replaces kid stuff in the house, and most kids complain that mom buys more dog toys and treats than she does human food and goodies. They buy Golden Retriever sweatshirts, jewelry, coasters and door knob covers. Friends wonder if they'll ever talk about anything except Goldens.

What makes people so crazy about their Golden Retrievers? It's simple, Goldens, more than any other breed, live to please their humans. Blessed with a loving disposition, a high degree of trainability, a most forgiving nature and an innate desire to make you

Did You Know? In 1908, the Golden Retriever appeared at one of the most famous dog exhibition events in Europe, called the Crystal Palace Dog Show, under the name "Flat Coat (Golden)."

happy, Goldens have captured a permanent corner of the American heart and home.

HUMBLE BEGINNINGS

As the youngest of the retriever breeds, Golden Retrievers have ruled our households for less than 100 years, a drop in the pond compared to most other breeds. Just where did this wonder breed come from? Those new to the breed may have heard the lively tale about the beautiful Russian tracking dogs that toured England with the circus. Don't believe a word of it. The real credit goes to a Scottish nobleman, the former Sir Dudley Majoribanks, who became the first Lord Tweedmouth of Guisachan in Inverness, Scotland.

Tweedmouth was a waterfowl enthusiast who hunted along the rugged English coast. He dreamed of a canine hunting partner possessed with a superb nose who would hunt closer than the commonly used setters and spaniels at that time. He also fancied a dog who would not only retrieve his birds, but deliver them to his hand, a dual talent that was lacking in the bird dogs of that era. In 1868, he bred a Wavy-Coated Retriever named Nous — a gift from the Earl of Chichester — to a liver-colored Tweed Water Spaniel named Belle, who had been given to Tweedmouth by his cousin, David Robertson.

Nous (the Greek word for "wisdom") was born the only yellow pup — then called a "sport" — out of a litter of all blacks coats, which was the standard color for the wavy coat, an ancestor of today's Flat-Coated Retriever. This choice was no accident; Tweedmouth had a passion for yellow dogs (a blessing for those who love those blond and reddish-gold coats).

Success! Belle produced four fuzzy yellow pups and thus launched Tweedmouth on his Golden journey. He kept his favorite pup and gave the others to a few good friends, who joined him in his breeding venture. (Read more about these humble beginnings in "Golden Days of Yore" on page 29.)

What a grand adventure it turned out to be. These Golden fanciers persisted, breeding yellow dog with yellow dog, despite that line breeding of this nature was uncommon at this time. Occasionally, they did experimental outcrosses to the Irish Setter, the yellow Labrador Retriever and the Bloodhound. (Where else could the expert Golden nose come from?)

The kennels at Guisachan were sold in 1905, but by that time two historic kennels (sometimes called "lines") had emerged: Ingestre and Culham, which were eventually registered with England's Kennel Club. Lord Harcourt's Culham Goldens continued

Just what is that "golden" color? Although it is difficult to tell from early photos, the original Golden Retrievers were a rich, yellow gold. Later Goldens tended toward a darker or even reddish gold, although some looked almost white. Today, the American Kennel Club breed standard specifically states that the coat should be a rich, lustrous gold and should not be "either extremely pale or extremely dark." Beyond that, your Golden Retriever can be any shade of gold between biscuit and bronze. Even if your pet is lighter or darker than the standard states that shouldn't affect her most important quality: that golden personality.

it's a Fact

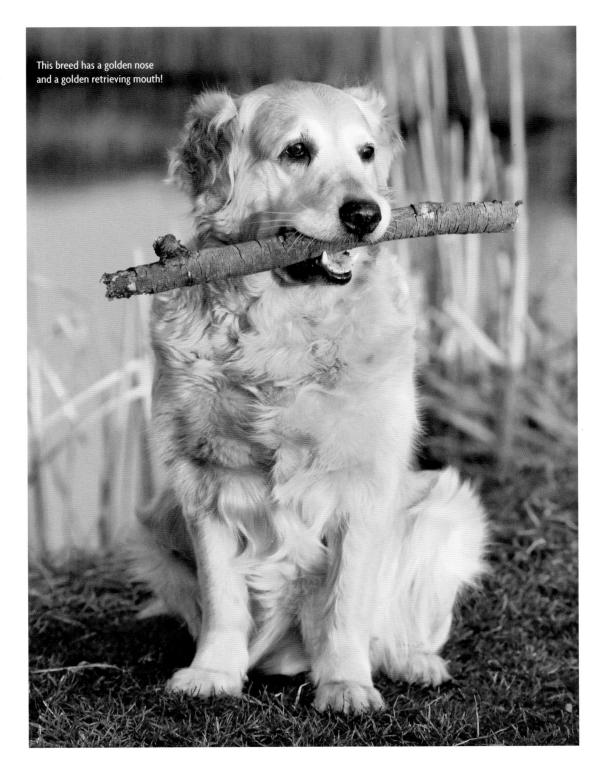

This breed has a golden nose and a golden retrieving mouth!

Tweedmouth's legacy of excellence, producing the great sires, Culham Brass and Culham Copper, the forbearers of the modern Golden Retriever.

In 1909, Lord Harcourt was joined in his breeding endeavors by Winifred Charlesworth, who later established her own line of influential Goldens under the kennel prefix Noranby (originally Noramby). Charlesworth became an icon for the breed, devoting the next 50 years to preserving the breed's working ability, always with an eye toward true type and soundness. Her Noranby Goldens not only worked admirably in the field but also claimed the highest honors on the bench, achievements not witnessed in the Golden Retriever for many decades. In 1913, she and a few other breed enthusiasts successfully formed the Golden Retriever Club of England.

The early 1900s were flagship years for the Golden Retriever in England. Goldens became a popular hunting dog, and the breed earned field trial wins and produced dual champions. Bench champions wore a darker red coat in those days, until about 1936 when the lighter colors became fashionable with judges and exhibitors.

OFFICIAL RECOGNITION

The Yellow Retriever, officially recognized by the English Kennel Club in 1913, became the Golden Retriever in 1920. The breed began migrating to Canada and the United States around 1900 when the British military and other professionals traveled to those countries with their dogs. By 1931, Goldens had also been exported to Uruguay, Belgium, Holland, India, South America, Kenya and Argentina — a true testimony to the breed's versatility and universal appeal.

Lord Tweedmouth's golden canine creation came to America in the late 19th century in the company of Lord Tweedmouth's son, the Honorable Archie Majoribanks, who lived on a Texas ranch with a Golden Retriever named Lady. At the time, few Americans knew about the breed, but that began to change in the 1920s, when a trend for all things British drove Americans to take notice of the Golden.

In 1925, Robert Appleton of Long Island, N.Y., registered the first Golden Retrievers with the American Kennel Club: Lomberdale Blondin and Dan Hill Judy. In 1939, fanciers primarily living in Minnesota and elsewhere in the Midwest formed the Golden Retriever Club of America.

When Word War II swept across Europe, many breeders, fearing for their dogs, sent them to the United States for protection, and American breeders benefited, producing many wonderful Golden Retrievers. The center of the Golden Retriever fancy remained in the Midwest for many years, but Canada also developed a fondness for the breed. The first Golden Retriever ever to win a Best In Show in the United States was Speedwell Pluto, an English import belonging to Col. Samuel Magoffin of Vancouver, British Columbia.

Pluto was also a talented hunting dog, and Magoffin had Midwestern ties, as well.

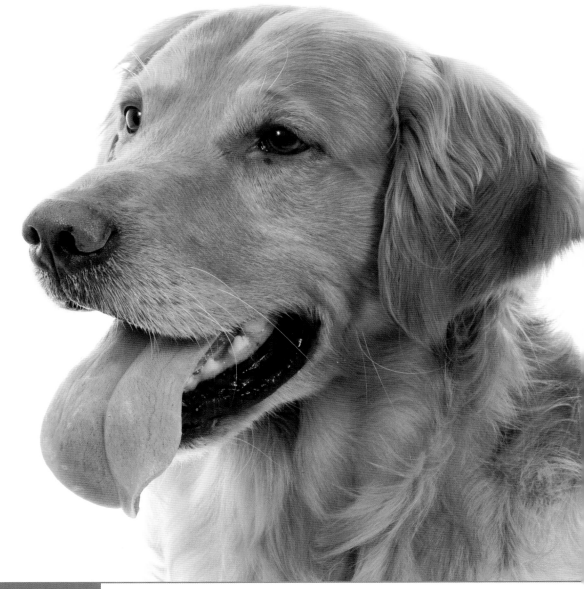

Goldens have been bred to be a sidekick or worker for the human being, and they have a wonderful work ethic. That work ethic lets them come across as sweet because they're biddable. They want to do what you ask; they don't necessarily have their own agenda like some independent working breeds. They were bred to be trainable.

— Laura Gibson, obedience competitor from Houston, Texas

His brother-in-law, Ralph Boalt of Minnesota, imported many Goldens from England, resulting in some of the most famous and accomplished field and show champions in America during the 1940s.

The Midwest has always been a hunter's paradise, so it's no wonder that Golden Retrievers excelled there. The first Golden Retriever in America to compete in organized field trials was a dog named Rip, a puppy from two English imports. Around this time, most Golden Retrievers were hunting dogs, but the more people got to know the beautiful, soft-coated, friendly-faced and trainable breed, the more they excelled in the show ring.

Some breeders worked to produce dogs that could best compete in dog shows, while others worked to refine the breed's hunting skills. Although many Golden Retrievers today can do well in show *and* field, many lines have diverged so that show and field lines barely resemble each other. Show dogs tend to be larger with a thicker coat, while field dogs tend to be smaller and more athletic with a thinner coat better suited for tearing through brush or bog. Casual weekend hunters enjoyed their Golden companions, and others chose to compete with their dogs in field trials.

NOT JUST FOR HUNTING ANYMORE

Today, Golden Retrievers contribute more to society than just a pretty face. Throughout the world, they serve their human partners as devoted guide dogs for the blind and hearing impaired, and expert assistance dogs for the physically disabled. In tandem with law enforcement agencies, they work in seaports, post offices, schools and prisons to sniff for drugs and other contraband. That same Golden talent works with the United States disaster teams to search for victims buried under snow or earthquake debris. As gentle and persuasive therapy dogs, they visit hospitals and nursing homes to lift the spirits of youngsters and seniors alike.

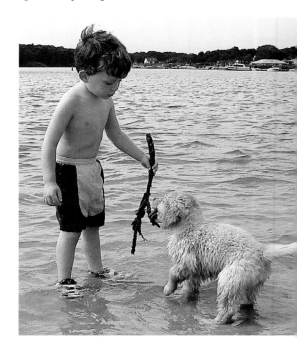

Golden Days of Yore

The puppy looked up at Sir Dudley Majoribanks from the floor of the cobbler's shop in southern England in 1865. The puppy had a coat of feathery gold and a wise expression. Majoribanks asked the cobbler about the dog and discovered that this one yellow pup in a litter of black Wavy-Coated Retrievers had been payment for a debt.

Majoribanks saw something in the dog, so he purchased the pup from the cobbler, named him Nous (which means "wisdom" in Greek) and took him home to Scotland.

Majoribanks, who later gained the title Lord Tweedmouth, kept large kennels of hunting dogs, but he wanted something specific from this yellow dog. In an age when black retrievers were the favorite, he wanted to create a unique hunting dog specifically to work over the rough terrain and in the harsh climate of the Scottish Highlands. He also preferred gold.

At the time, there wasn't a dog called Golden Retriever, but Wavy-Coated Retrievers were popular hunters all over the British Isles. In 1868, and again in 1871, Lord Tweedmouth bred Nous to a female Tweed Water Spaniel named Belle. Extinct today, the Tweed Water Spaniel was a hearty and hard-working breed with a strong instinct for water retrieving and a weather-proof coat. Four beautiful, yellow females came out of these two matings: Crocus, Cowslip, Primrose and Ada.

Fortunately for those interested in the precise pedigrees of their Golden Retrievers, Lord Tweedmouth kept exact records of all breedings, which included other Wavy-Coated Retrievers, Tweed Water Spaniels and Irish Setters (or "Red Setters"). No matter what combinations Lord Tweedmouth tried in order to tweak the breed, he always chose the yellow puppies (and occasionally black ones with admirable traits) to establish his new breed. Some people also believe other breeds may have contributed to the Golden we know today, including a small Newfoundland and a Bloodhound.

Lord Tweedmouth's very last entry noted a mating between a second Nous (a descendent of the original) and a female named Queenie, resulting in two golden female puppies, named Prim and Rose. If you could look back far enough into the pedigrees of most Golden Retrievers today, you should find these two Golden girls. And so the Golden Retriever — although not named yet — was born.

For an all-around, hunting dog, the Golden has it all. Athletic and willing, this retriever is easy to train and happy to spend a whole day hunting with his human companions. Although most Goldens today don't hunt but work as family pets instead, Goldens bred specifically for hunting — and even some bred for other purposes — have a natural instinct for finding the bird and bringing it back.

As competitors, Goldens dazzle audiences wherever they perform. They dance around the show ring, knock out the competition in the obedience ring and fulfill their heritage in hunting tests and field trials. In agility events, these all-around athletes easily outperform other breeds, streaking through the obstacle course with their usual sporting panache. Tracking? That Golden nose is one of their most famous traits, it's no wonder more Golden Retrievers earn tracking titles annually than any other breed. In fact, almost every canine activity and sporting discipline boasts one or more Golden overachievers in the record book.

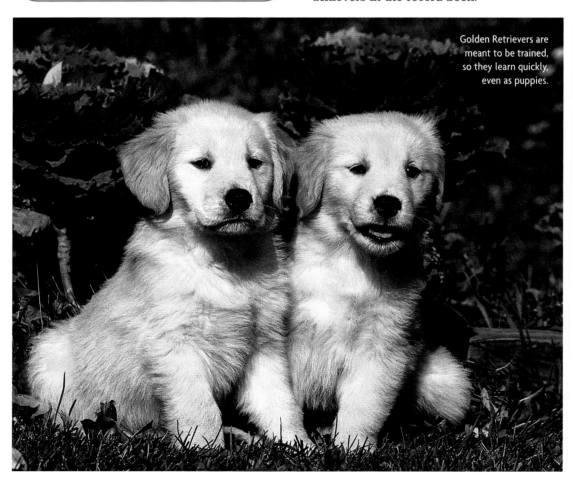

Golden Retrievers are meant to be trained, so they learn quickly, even as puppies.

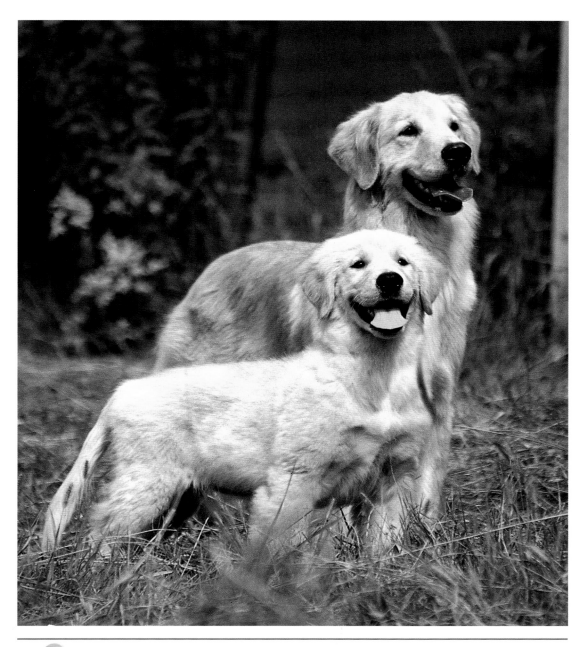

You have an unbreakable bond with your dog, but do you always understand him? Go online and download "Dog Speak," which outlines how dogs communicate. Find out what your Golden Retriever is saying when he barks, howls or growls. Go to **DogChannel.com/Club-Gold** and click on "Downloads."

Yet the most prominent role of the 21st century Golden Retriever is that of family companion and devoted friend. On the home front, they are the most loyal companions, playing with the kids and clearing the yard of fallen sticks and branches. You can usually identify a Golden Retriever's home by the huge pile of retrieved sticks piled up at the front door. Lord Tweedmouth would be very pleased.

Unfortunately, it is that unique combination of huggability, talent and trainability that makes such diversification possible, which also makes the Golden the ideal candidate for dissent and separation within the ranks of breeders and exhibitors. This breed schism is old news; these same concerns existed 50 years ago, but today they're more pronounced due to the increase in the Golden population. Particularly during the past three decades, the breed has splintered into specific lines bred to excel in conformation, field work or obedience.

Each of these disciplines has become so specialized that many fanciers have lost sight of the "complete and correct" Golden as they pursue their "ideal" Golden. Today's competitors frequently breed and promote the type of dog best suited to their particular interest: conformation work, field dogs or obedience. Conformation dogs are bred with heavy bone and still heavier coats, and are physically and mentally unable to spend even a few hours in the field. Field dogs are bred purely for function and look like distant relatives of the traditional Golden. Obedience dogs are bred to have so much go-power that they border hyperactive. Goldens in each area are bred without regard for the true Golden temperament or original purpose. The superior talent that has evolved with such breeding practices has only expanded the market for specialized Goldens.

Veterinarians today see too many Goldens who are hyper, testy and even aggressive, which are far from the temperament standard. They also see health problems such as immune deficiencies, weak hips, allergies and much more, as a result of indiscriminate breeding practices. Lord Tweedmouth would be heartbroken.

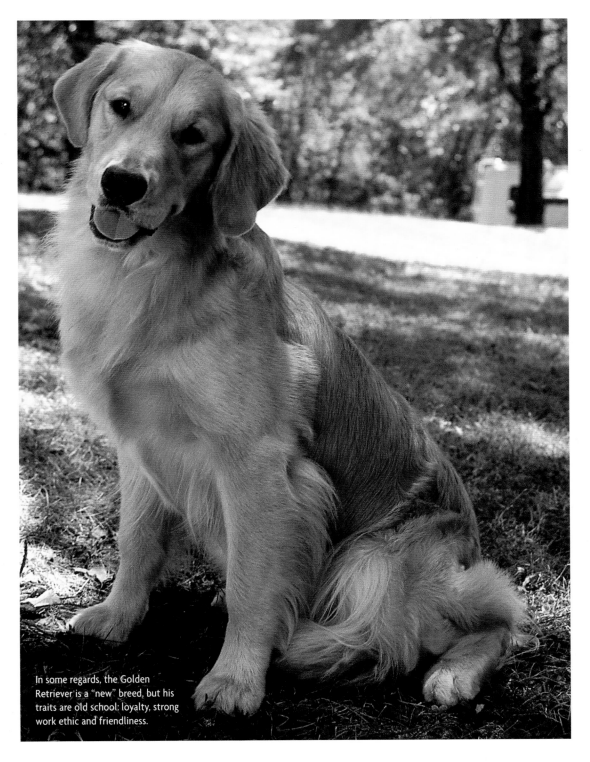

In some regards, the Golden Retriever is a "new" breed, but his traits are old school: loyalty, strong work ethic and friendliness.

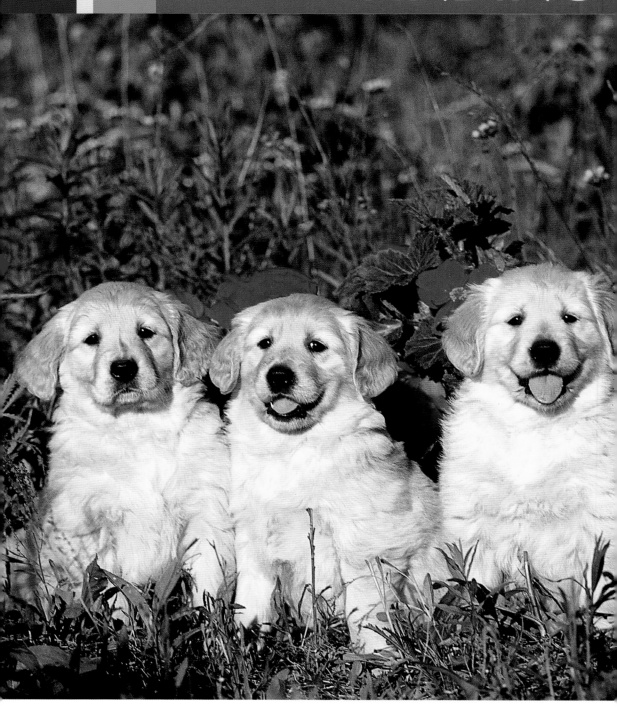

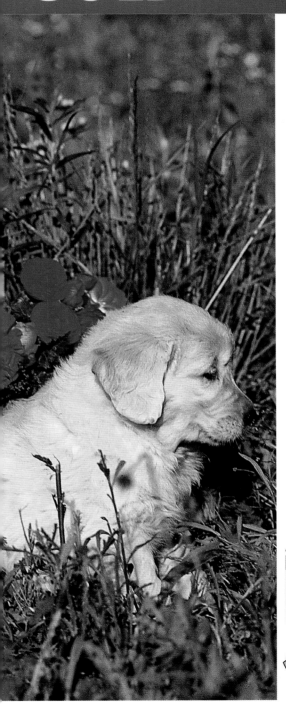

As rough and tumble as the Golden Retriever can be, nothing is cuter than a Golden puppy. His sweet face and round little body inspire *oohs* and *ahhs* from all who see him. That wonderful endearing quality, however, can also distract you from taking the time and doing the legwork necessary to find a puppy who's not only adorable, but also healthy in body and temperament. The key to finding the best Golden Retriever puppy for you is to resist being charmed into a hasty decision and wait to find a responsible breeder. Then, you can have fun picking the right puppy from a litter of those lovable faces.

You're going to have your dog for 10 to 12 years, so the time you spend early on to locate a healthy, well-adjusted Golden puppy from a reputable breeder will definitely pay off in the long run. Look for a dedicated and ethical breeder who values good health and stable personalities, and who really cares what happens to the dog for the rest of his life.

Why is this so important? This is a breed with a unique personality who needs to be

it's a Fact

Local breeder referrals are essential. A breeder who belongs to a local Golden Retriever club shows active involvement in the breed and breeds according to that club's code of ethics. That's who you want to do business with: a breeder who abides by a code of ethics.

bred correctly by someone with experience and really knows what he or she is doing. If not, you may wind up with a dog who's overly aggressive, has a number of health problems and doesn't even look like a true Golden.

Be sure to avoid puppy mills and backyard breeders. Puppy mills are large-scale breeding operations that produce puppies in an assembly-line fashion without regard to health and socialization. Backyard breeders are typically well-meaning, regular pet owners who simply don't possess enough knowledge about the breed and breeding to produce healthy puppies.

The American Kennel Club and the United Kennel Club provide a list of breeders in good standing with their organizations. Visit their websites for more information (see Resources section on page 166 for contact information).

EVALUATING BREEDERS

Once you have the names and numbers of breeders in your area, start contacting them to find out more about their breeding programs. Before you contact them, prepare some questions to ask that will get you the important information you need to know.

Prospective buyers interview breeders much the same way that a breeder should interview a buyer. Record the answers you receive so you can compare them to the answers from other breeders whom you may interview later. The right questions are those that help you identify who has been involved with the breed a respectable number of years and who is actively showing their dogs. Ask in-depth questions regarding the genetic health of the parents, grandparents and great grandparents of any puppy you are considering. Ask what sort of genetic testing program the breeder adheres to.

Look to see if a breeder actively shows his or her dogs in conformation events (dog shows). Showing indicates that the breeder is bringing out examples from his or her breeding program for the public to see. If there are any obvious problems, such as temperament or general conformation, they will be readily apparent. Also, the main reason to breed Golden Retrievers is to improve the quality of the breed. If the breeder is not showing, then he or she is more likely to be breeding purely for monetary reasons and may have less concern for the welfare and future of the breed.

Inquiring about health and determining the breeder's willingness to work with you in the future are also important for the potential puppy buyer to learn. Research what kind of health guarantees the breeder gives. You should also find out if the breeder will be available for future consultation regarding your Golden, and find out if the breeder will take your dog back if something unforeseen happens.

Prospective buyers should ask plenty of questions, and in return buyers should also be prepared to answer questions posed by a responsible breeder who wants to make sure his or her puppy is going to a good home. Be prepared for a battery of questions from the

Did You Know?

Good Breeder Signs When you visit a Golden Retriever breeder, look around the home for:
- a clean, well-maintained facility
- no overwhelming odors
- an overall impression of cleanliness
- socialized dogs and puppies

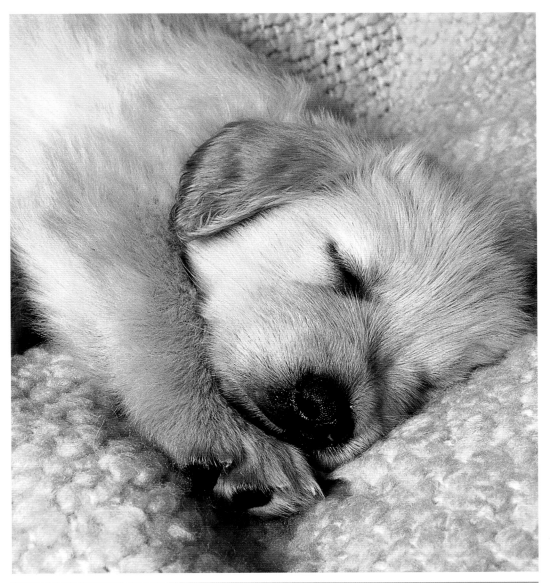

NOTABLE & QUOTABLE

Golden Retrievers are gun dogs, retrievers bred for hard work and long hours in the field retrieving shot game. As such, they tend to have a strong retrieve drive, and some are fanatical retrievers, constantly retrieving items for their owners.

— Anne McGuire of Katy, Texas, former puppy referral coordinator for the Golden Retriever Club of America

breeder regarding your purpose for wanting this breed of dog and whether you can properly care for one. Avoid buying from a breeder who does little or no screening. If a breeder doesn't ask any questions, they are not concerned with where their pups end up. In this case, the dogs' best interests are probably not the breeder's motive for breeding.

Find a breeder who is willing to answer any questions and is knowledgeable about the history of the breed, health issues and about the background of their own dogs. Learn about a breeder's long-term commitment to the Golden Retriever breed and to their puppies after they leave the kennel.

Look for breeders who know their purpose for producing a particular litter, those who are knowledgeable in the pedigrees of their dogs and of the Golden Retriever breed itself and have had the necessary health screenings performed on the parents. They should also ask you for references to show that they are interested in establishing a relationship with you in consideration for a puppy. If after one phone conversation with a breeder, the person is supplying you with an address in which to send a deposit, continue your search for a reputable breeder elsewhere.

Did You Know?

Healthy puppies have clear eyes, shiny coats, and are playful and friendly. An important factor in a puppy's long-term health and good temperament is the age he goes to his permanent home, which should be between 8 and 10 weeks. This gives the puppies plenty of time to develop immunity and bond with their mother.

CHOOSING THE RIGHT PUP

Once you have found a breeder you are comfortable with, your next step is to pick the right puppy. The good news is that if you have done your homework and found a responsible breeder, you can count on this person to give you plenty of help in choosing the right pup for your personality and lifestyle. In fact, most good breeders will recommend a specific puppy once they know what kind of dog you want.

After you have narrowed down the search and selected a reputable breeder, rely on the experience of the breeder to help you select your puppy. The selection of the puppy depends a lot on what purpose the pup is being purchased for. If the pup is being purchased as a show prospect, the breeder will offer their assessment of the pups that meet this criteria and be able to explain the strengths and faults of each.

Whether your Golden puppy is show or pet quality, a good, stable temperament is vital for a happy relationship. Generally, you want to avoid a timid puppy or a very dominant one. Temperament is very important, and a reputable breeder should spend a lot of time with the pups and be able to offer an evaluation of each pup's personality. A reputable breeder might tell you which Golden Retriever puppy is appropriate for your home and personality. They may not allow you to choose the puppy, although they certainly will take your preference into consideration.

Some breeders, on the other hand, believe it's important for you to be heavily involved in selecting a puppy from the litter. They will let the buyers make the decision on which pup to take home because not everyone is looking for the same things in a dog. Some people want a quiet, laidback attitude. Others want an outgoing, active dog. When pups are old enough to go to their

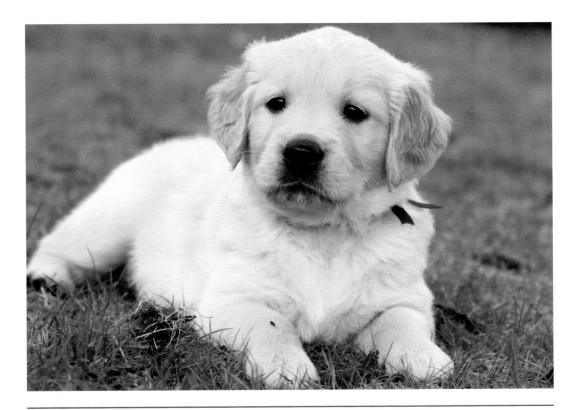

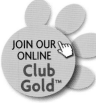

Questions to Expect
Be prepared for the breeder to ask you some questions, too.

1. Have you previously owned a Golden Retriever?

The breeder is trying to gauge how familiar you are with the breed. If you have never owned one, illustrate your knowledge of Goldens by telling the breeder about your research.

2. Do you have children? What are their ages?

Some breeders are wary about selling a dog to families with younger children. This isn't a steadfast rule, and some breeders insist on meeting the children to see how they handle puppies. It all depends on the breeder.

3. How long have you wanted a Golden Retriever?

This helps a breeder know if this purchase is an impulse buy or a carefully thought-out decision. Buying on impulse is one of the biggest mistakes owners can make. Be patient.

Join Club Gold to get a complete list of questions a breeder should ask you. Click on "Downloads" at: **DogChannel.com/Club-Gold**

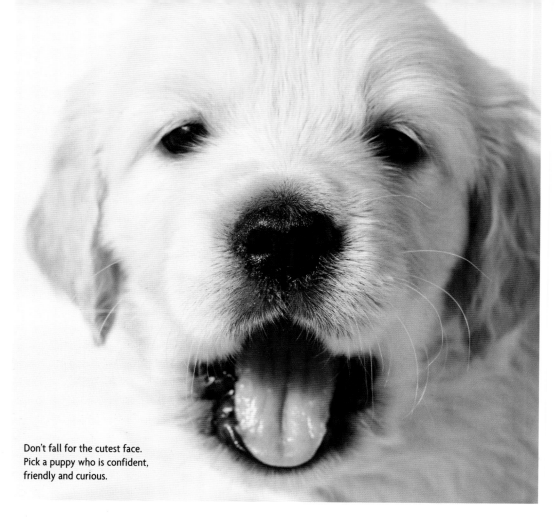

Don't fall for the cutest face.
Pick a puppy who is confident,
friendly and curious.

new homes (roughly 8 to 10 weeks), some breeders prefer for you make the decision because no one can tell at this age which puppy will make the most intelligent or affectionate dog. The color, sex and markings are obvious, but that is about all you can tell for sure at this age. With everything else being equal, some breeders suggest picking the puppy whom you have a gut feeling for.

The chemistry between a buyer and puppy is important and should play a role in determining which pup goes to which home. When possible, make numerous visits to see the puppies, and in effect, let a puppy choose you. There usually will be one puppy who spends more time with a buyer and is more comfortable relaxing and sitting with or on a person.

CHECKING FOR GOLDEN QUALITIES

Whether you are dealing with a breeder who wants to pick a pup for you or lets you make the decision alone, consider certain points when evaluating the pup you may end up calling your own. The puppy should be friendly and outgoing, not skittish in any way, and he should be forgiving of correction. He shouldn't be too terribly mouthy. The pup should readily follow you and be willing to snuggle in your lap and be turned onto his back easily without a problem.

With the popularity of Golden Retrievers, shelters and rescue groups across the country are often inundated with sweet, loving examples of the breed — from the tiniest puppies to senior dogs,

petite females to strapping males. Often, to get the Golden Retriever of your dreams, it takes a trip to the local shelter. Or, perhaps you could find your ideal dog waiting patiently in the arms of a foster parent at a nearby rescue group. It just takes a bit of effort, patience and a willingness to find the right dog for your family, not just the cutest dog on the block.

The perks of owning a Golden are plentiful: companionship, unconditional love, true loyalty and laughter, just to name a few. So why choose the adoption option? Because you will literally be saving a life!

Owners of adopted dogs swear they're more grateful and loving than any dog they've owned before. It's almost as if they knew what dire fate awaited them and are so thankful to you. Goldens, known for their people-pleasing personalities, seem to embody this mentality wholeheartedly when they're rescued. And they want to give something back. Another perk: Almost all adopted dogs come fully vetted, with proper medical treatment and vaccinations, as well as being spayed or neutered. Some are even licensed and microchipped.

Don't disregard older dogs by thinking the only good pair-up is between you and a puppy. Adult Goldens are more established behaviorally and personality-wise, helping to better mesh their characteristics with yours in this game of matchmaker. Puppies are always in high demand, so if you open your options to include adults, you will have a better chance of adopting quickly. Plus, adult dogs are often housetrained, calmer, chew-proof and don't need to be taken outside in the middle of the night ... five times ... in the pouring rain.

The Golden Retriever Club of America offers rescue support information or log onto Petfinder.com. The site's searchable database allows you to find a Golden in your area who needs a break in the form of a compassionate owner like you. More websites are listed in the Resources chapter on page 166.

Proper temperament is very important. A Golden Retriever puppy who has a dominant personality requires an experienced owner who will be firm during training. A puppy who is a little shy requires heavy socialization to build his confidence.

You also can evaluate a Golden puppy's temperament on your own. The temperament of the pups can be evaluated by spending some time watching them. If you can visit the pups and observe them first together with their littermates, then you can see how they interact with each other. You may be able to pinpoint which ones are the bullies and which ones are more submissive. In general, look for a puppy who is more interested in you than in his littermates. Then, take each pup individually to a new location away from the rest of the litter. Put the puppy down on the ground, walk away and see how he reacts away from the security of his littermates. The puppy may be afraid at first, but he should gradually recover and start checking out his new surroundings

D-I-Y TEMPERAMENT TEST

Puppies come in a wide assortment of temperaments to suit almost everyone. If you are looking for a dog who is easily trainable and a good companion to your family, you most likely want a puppy with a medium temperament.

Temperament testing can help you determine the type of disposition your potential puppy possesses. A pup with a medium temperament will have the following reactions to these tests, best conducted when the pup is 7 weeks old.

Step 1. To test a pup's social attraction and his confidence in approaching humans, coax him toward you by kneeling down and clapping your hands gently. A pup with a medium temperament comes readily, tail up or down.

Step 2. To test a pup's eagerness to follow, walk away from him while he is watching you. He should follow you readily, tail up.

Step 3. To see how a pup handles restraint, kneel down and roll the pup gently on his back. Using a light but firm touch, hold him in this position with one hand for

---

Breeder Q&A

JOIN OUR ONLINE **Club Gold™**

Here are some questions you should ask a breeder and the answers you want.

Q. How often do you have litters available?

A. You want to hear "once or twice a year" or "occasionally" because a breeder who doesn't have litters that often is probably more concerned with the quality of his puppies, rather than with making money.

Q. What kinds of health problems do Goldens have?

A. Beware of a breeder who says, "none." Every breed has health issues. For Golden Retrievers, some health problems include cataracts, ectropion, entropion, heart disease, hip dysplasia and cancer.

Get a complete list of questions to ask a Golden breeder — and the correct answers — at Club Gold. Log onto **DogChannel.com/Club-Gold** and click on "Downloads."

30 seconds. The Golden Retriever puppy should settle down after some initial struggle and offer some or steady eye contact.

Step 4. To evaluate a puppy's level of social dominance, stand up, then crouch down beside the pup and stroke him from head to back. A Golden puppy with a medium temperament — neither too dominant nor too submissive — should cuddle up to you and lick your face, or squirm and lick your hands.

Step 5. An additional test of a pup's dominance level is to bend over, cradle the pup under his belly with your fingers interlaced and palms up, and elevate him just off the ground. Hold him there for 30 seconds. The pup should not struggle and should be relaxed, or he should struggle and then settle down and lick you.

PHYSICAL FEATURES

To assess a puppy's health, take a deliberate, thorough look at each part of his body. Signs of a healthy puppy include

bright eyes, a healthy coat, a good appetite and firm stool.

Watch for a telltale link between physical and mental health. A healthy Golden Retriever, as with any breed, will display a happier, more positive attitude than an unhealthy puppy. A Golden Retriever puppy's belly should not be over extended or hard, as this may be a sign of worms. If you are

When visiting a breeder, make sure to see the puppies when they are awake.

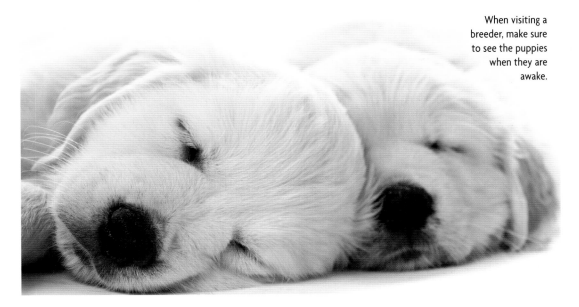

Food intolerance is a dog's inability to completely digest certain foods. Puppies who may have done very well on their mother's milk may not do well on cow's milk. The result of this food intolerance may be loose bowels, passing gas and stomach pains. These are the only obvious symptoms of food intolerance, which makes diagnosis difficult.

around the litter long enough to witness a bowel movement, the stool should be solid and the pup should not show any signs of discomfort. Look into the pup's eyes, too; they should be bright and full of life.

When purchasing a Golden puppy, buyers hear from breeders that these dogs are just like any other puppy — times 10! They are very smart, loving, sometimes stubborn and often have their own agendas. If a prospective owner isn't willing to spend a fair amount of time with a Golden, then the breed is not for them. A Golden Retriever wants to

be with people and is quite similar to a 7-year-old boy in the sense that he needs attention and consistent reinforcement for behavioral parameters. Once through adolescence, however, a Golden is the best friend, guardian and companion a person or family could have.

PUPPY PARTICULARS

Here are signs to look for when picking a puppy from a breeder. When in doubt, ask the breeder which puppy they think has the best personality/temperament to fit your lifestyle.

1. Look at the area where the pups spend most of their time. It's OK if they play outdoors part of the day, but they should sleep indoors at night so the pups can interact with people and become accustomed to hearing ordinary household noises. This will build a solid foundation for a well-socialized Golden puppy. The puppies' area should be clean and well lit.

2. Sure, you're only buying one puppy, but make sure to see all of the puppies in the litter. By 5 weeks of age, healthy pups will begin playing with one another and should be lively and energetic. It's OK if they're asleep when you visit, but stay long

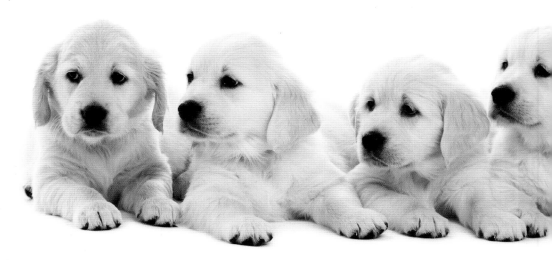

enough to see them wake up. Once they're up, they shouldn't be lethargic or weak, as this may be a sign of illness.

3. Puppies should be confident and eager to greet you. A pup who is shy and stays in the corner may be insecure. Although some introverted pups come out of their shells later on, many do not. These dogs will be fearful as adults and are not good choices for an active, noisy family, with or without children, or for people who have never owned a dog. They require a tremendous amount of training and social-ization in order to live a happy life.

Choose a Golden puppy who is happy and eager to interact with you but reject the ones who are either too shy or too bossy. These extreme temperament types are a challenge to deal with, and require a lot of training to socialize. The perfect Golden Retriever puppy personality is somewhere between the two extremes.

4. If it's feeding time during your visit, all pups should be eager to gobble up their food. A puppy who refuses to eat may have an illness.

5. The dog's skin should be smooth, clean and shiny without any sores or bumps. Puppies should not be biting or scratching at themselves continuously, as this could signal fleas.

6. After 10 to 12 days, eyes should be open and clear without any redness or discharges. Pups should not be scratching at their eyes, as this may cause an infection or signal irritation.

7. Vomiting or coughing more than once is not normal. If so, a Golden Retriever puppy might be ill and should visit the vet-erinarian immediately.

8. Visit long enough to see the Golden Retriever pups eliminate. All stools should be firm without being watery or bloody. These are signs of illness or that a puppy has worms.

9. Golden Retriever puppies should walk or run freely without limping.

10. A healthy Golden puppy who is getting enough to eat should not be skinny. You should be able to slightly feel his ribs if you rub his abdomen, but you should not be able to see his ribs protruding.

On the outside, puppies in a litter can look exactly the same. That's why a smart owner will let the breeder select a puppy with the right temperament to fit the owner's lifestyle.

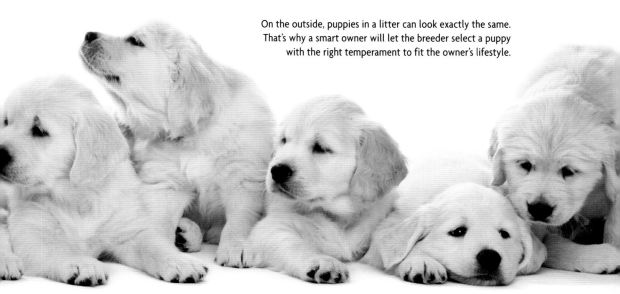

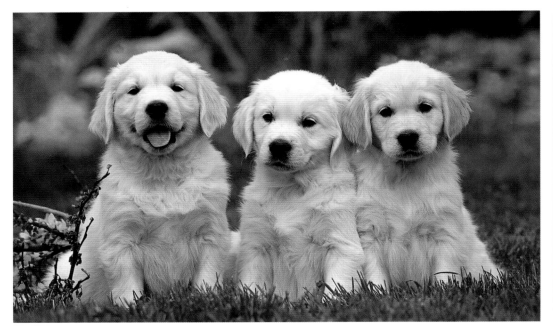

BREEDER PAPERS

Everything today comes with an instruction manual. When you purchase a Golden Retriever puppy, it's no different. A reputable breeder should give you a registration application; a sales contract; a health guarantee; your puppy's complete health records; a three-, four- or five-generation pedigree; and some general information on behavior, care, conformation, health and training.

Healthy Puppy Signs

Here are a few things you should look for when selecting a puppy from a litter.

1. NOSE: It should be slightly moist to the touch, but there shouldn't be excessive discharge. The puppy should not be persistently sneezing or sniffling.

2. SKIN AND COAT: A Golden puppy's coat should be soft and shiny, without flakes or excessive shedding. Watch out for patches of missing hair, redness, bumps or sores. The pup should have a pleasant smell. Check for parasites, such as fleas or ticks.

3. BEHAVIOR: A healthy Golden pup may be sleepy, but she should not be lethargic. A healthy puppy will be playful at times, not isolated in a corner. You should see occasional bursts of energy and interaction with her littermates. At mealtime, a healthy puppy will take an interest in her food.

There are more signs to look for when picking out the perfect Golden Retriever puppy for your lifestyle. Download the list at **DogChannel.com/Club-Gold**

Registration Application. This document from the AKC or UKC assigns your puppy a number and identifies the dog by listing his date of birth, identifying the names of his parents and showing that he is registered as a purebred Golden. It doesn't prove whether or not your dog is a show- or a pet-quality Golden and doesn't provide any health guarantee.

Sales Contract. A reputable breeder should discuss the terms of the contract with you before asking you to sign it. This is a written understanding of both of your expectations and shows that the breeder cares about the pup's welfare throughout his life. The contract can include such terms as requiring you to keep the dog indoors at night, spaying or neutering if the puppy is not going to be a show dog, providing routine vet care and assurance that you'll feed your dog a healthy diet. Most responsible breeders will ask that you take your dog to obedience classes and earn a Canine Good Citizen title (an AKC training certification for dogs that exhibit good manners) before he is 2 years old. Many breeders also require new owners to have totally secure fencing and gates around their yard. Golden Retrievers are incredible escape artists, and they will find a way out of the yard if there's even the slightest opening.

Health Guarantee. This includes a letter from a veterinarian stating that the puppy has been examined and is healthy. It also states that the breeder will replace your dog if he develops a genetic, life-threatening illness during his lifetime.

Health Records. This is everything you want to know about your puppy's and his parents' health. It should include the dates the puppy was vaccinated, dewormed and examined by a veterinarian for signs of heart murmur, plus the parents' test results for the presence or absence of hip and elbow dysplasia, heart problems and luxated patellas.

Pedigree. Breeders should provide you with a copy of the puppy's three-, four- or five-generation pedigree. Many breeders also have photos of the dog's ancestors that they will proudly share with you.

Extra Information. The best breeders pride themselves on handing over a notebook full of the latest information on Golden behavior, care, conformation, health and training. Be sure to read it because it will provide valuable help while raising your Golden Retriever.

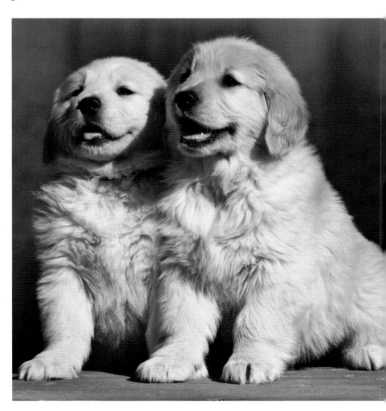

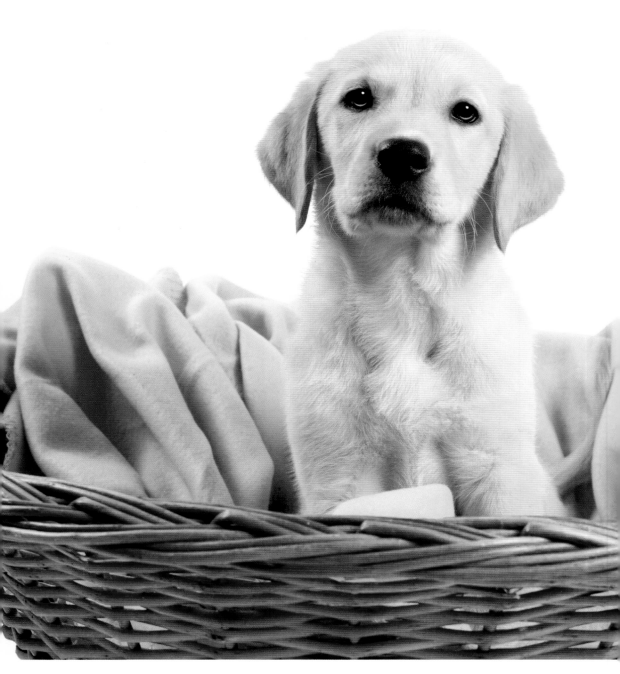

ESSENTIALS

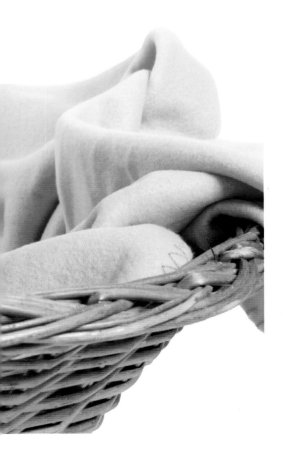

Don't for one second think that a Golden Retriever would prefer to live out in the golden sunshine. He, like every other breed, wants to live in the best accommodations with plenty of toys, soft bedding and other luxuries. Your home is now his home, too; and, before you even bring that new puppy or rescue dog into his new forever home, be a smart owner and make your home accessible for him.

In fact, in order for him to grow into a stable, well-adjusted dog, he has to feel comfortable in his surroundings. Remember, he is leaving the warmth and security of his mother and littermates, as well as the familiarity of the only place he has ever known, so it is important to make his transition to your home — his new home — as easy as possible.

PUPPY-PROOFING

Aside from making sure that your Golden will be comfortable in your home, you also have to ensure that your home is safe, which means taking the proper precautions to keep your pup away from things that are dangerous for him.

it's a Fact

Dangers lurk indoors and outdoors. Keep your curious Golden from investigating your shed and garage. Antifreeze and fertilizers, such as those you would use for roses, can kill any dog. Keep these items on high shelves that are out of reach.

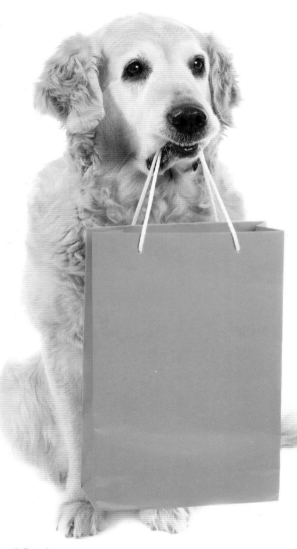

SMART TIP!

A well-stocked toy box should contain three main categories of toys.
1. **action** — anything that you can throw or roll and get things moving
2. **distraction** — durable toys that make dogs work for a treat
3. **comfort** — soft, stuffed "security blankets"

Puppy-proof your home inside and out before bringing your Golden Retriever home for the first time. Place breakables out of reach. If he is limited to certain places within the house, keep potentially dangerous items in off-limit areas. If your Golden is going to spend time in a crate, make sure that there isn't anything near it that he can reach if he sticks his curious little nose or paws through the openings.

The outside of your home must also be safe. Your pup will want to run and explore the yard, and he should be granted that freedom — as long as you are there to supervise. Do not let a fence give you a false sense of security; you would be surprised how crafty and persistent a Golden Retriever puppy can be in figuring out how to dig under a fence or squeeze his way through holes. The remedy is to make the fence well-embedded into the ground. Be sure to repair or secure any gaps in the fence. Check the fence periodically to ensure that it is in good shape and make repairs as needed; a very determined puppy may work on the same spot until he is able to get through.

The following are a few common problem areas to watch out for in the home and yard.

■ **Electrical cords and wiring:** No electrical cord or wiring is safe. Many office-supply stores sell products to keep wires gathered under computer desks, as well as products that prevent office chair wheels (and puppy teeth) from damaging electrical cords. If you have exposed cords and wires, these products aren't very expensive and can be used to keep a puppy out of trouble.

■ **Trash cans:** Don't waste your time trying to train your Golden not to get into the trash. Put the garbage behind a cabinet door and use a child-safe lock, if necessary. Dogs love bathroom trash, which consists of items that are hazardous (e.g., cotton balls, cotton

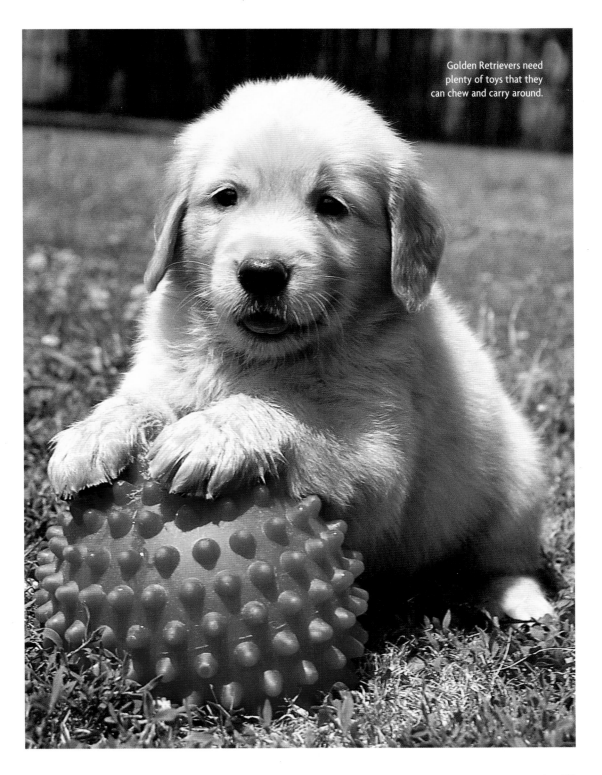

Golden Retrievers need plenty of toys that they can chew and carry around.

swabs, used razors, dental floss, etc.). Put the bathroom trash can in a cabinet under the sink and make sure you always shut the door to the bathroom.

■ **Household cleaners:** Make sure your Golden Retriever puppy doesn't have access to any of these deadly chemicals. Keep them behind closed cabinet doors, using child-safe locks, if necessary.

■ **Pest control sprays and poisons:** Chemicals to control ants or other pests should never be used in the house, if possible. Your Golden pup doesn't have to directly ingest these poisons to become ill; if he steps in the poison, he can experience toxic effects by licking his paws. Roach motels and other toxic pest traps are also yummy to dogs, so don't drop these behind couches or cabinets; if there's room for a roach motel, there's room for a determined Golden.

■ **Fabric:** Here's one you might not think about: Some puppies have a habit of licking blankets, upholstery, rugs or carpets. Though this habit seems fairly innocuous, over time the fibers from the upholstery or carpet can accumulate in the dog's stomach and cause a blockage. If you see your dog licking these items, remove the item or prevent him from having contact with it.

■ **Prescriptions, painkillers, supplements and vitamins:** Keep all medications in a cabinet. Also, be very careful when taking your prescription medications, supplements or vitamins: How often have you dropped a pill? You can be sure that your Golden puppy will be in between your legs and will grab the pill before you even start to say "No!" Dispense your pills carefully and without your Golden Retriever present.

■ **Miscellaneous loose items:** If it's not bolted to the floor, your puppy is likely to give the item a taste test. Socks, coins, children's toys, game pieces, cat toys — you name it. If it's on the floor, it's worth a try. Make sure the floors in your home are picked up and free of clutter.

FAMILY INTRODUCTIONS

Everyone in the house will be excited about the puppy's homecoming and will want to pet and play with him, but it is best to make the introduction low-key as not to overwhelm your puppy. He will already be apprehensive. It is the first time he has been separated from his mother, littermates and breeder and the ride to your home is likely to be the first time he has been in a car. The last thing you want to do is smother your pup, as this will only frighten him further. This is not to say that human contact is unnecessary at this stage because this is the time when a connection between the pup and his human family is formed. Gentle petting and soothing words should help console your Golden, as well as putting him down and letting him explore on his own (under your watchful eye, of course).

Your pup may approach the family members or may busy himself with exploring for a while. Gradually, each person should spend some time with the pup, one at a time, crouching down to get as close to the Golden's level as possible, letting him sniff their hands before petting him gently. He

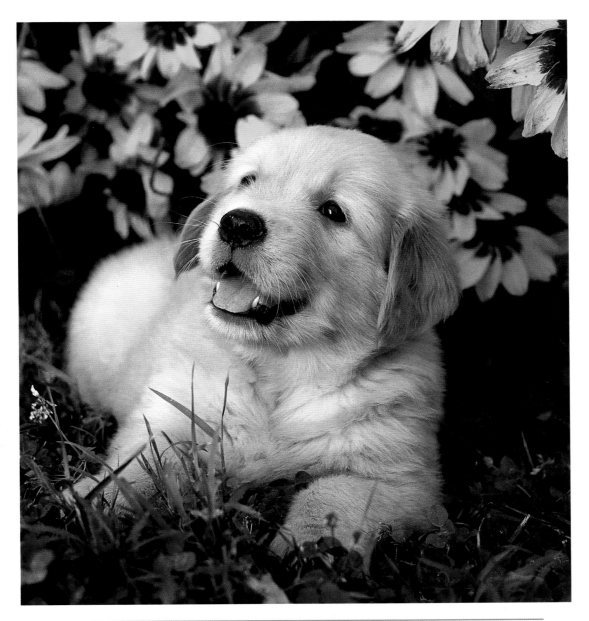

NOTABLE & QUOTABLE

The first thing you should always do before your puppy comes home is to lie on the ground and look around. You want to be able to see everything your puppy is going to see. For the puppy, the world is one big chew toy.

— Cathleen Stamm, rescue volunteer in San Diego, Calif.

definitely needs human attention, and he needs to be touched; this is how to form an immediate bond with your new Golden Retriever. Just remember that the puppy is experiencing a lot of things for the first time, all at once. There are new people, new noises, new smells and lots of new things to investigate. Be gentle, be affectionate and especially be as comforting as you can possibly be.

PUP'S FIRST NIGHT HOME

You have traveled home with your new puppy safely in his crate. He may have already been to the vet for a thorough check-up — he's been weighed, his papers examined, perhaps he's even been vaccinated and dewormed as well. Your Golden has met and licked the whole family, including the excited children and the less-than-happy cat. He's explored his area, his new bed, the

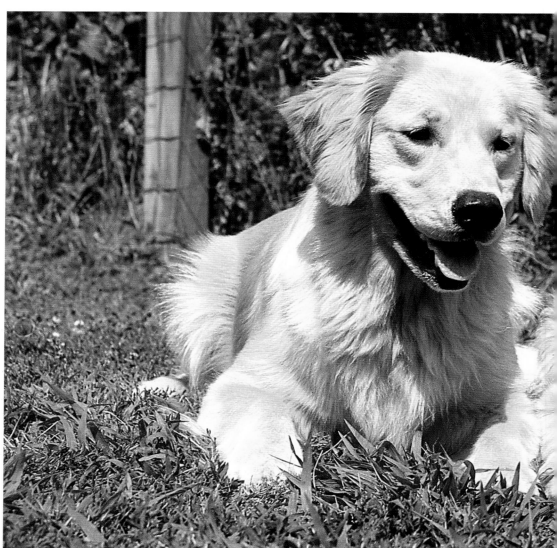

yard and everywhere else he's permitted. He's eaten his first meal at home and relieved himself in the proper place. Your Golden has heard lots of new sounds, smelled new friends and seen more of the outside world than ever before. This was just the first day! He's worn out and is ready for bed — or so you think!

Remember, this is your puppy's first night to sleep alone. His mother and littermates

SMART TIP!

When you are unable to watch your Golden Retriever puppy, put her in a crate or an exercise pen on an easily cleanable floor. If she has an accident on carpeting, clean it completely and meticulously, so that it doesn't smell like her potty forever.

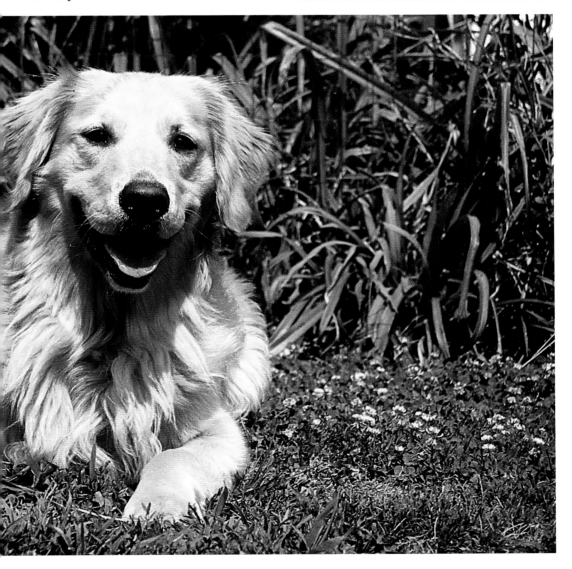

are no longer at paw's length, and he's scared, cold and lonely. Be reassuring to your new family member. This is not the time to spoil your Golden and give in to his inevitable whining.

Puppies whine. They whine to let others know where they are and hopefully to get company out of it. Place your Golden puppy in his new bed or crate in his room and close the door. Mercifully, he may fall asleep without a peep. If the inevitable occurs, ignore the whining; he is fine. Do not give in and visit your Golden puppy. He will fall asleep eventually.

Many breeders recommend placing a piece of bedding from his former home in his new bed so that he will recognize the scent of his littermates. Others advise placing a hot water bottle in his bed for warmth. The latter may be a good idea provided the pup doesn't attempt to suckle.

Your Golden Retriever's first night can be somewhat terrifying for him. Remember that you set the tone of nighttime at your house. Unless you want to play with your pup every night at 10 p.m., midnight and 2 a.m., don't initiate the habit. Your family will thank you, and so will your pup!

PET-SUPPLY STORE SHOPPING

It's fun shopping for new things for a new puppy. From training to feeding and sleeping to playing, your new Golden Retriever will need a few items to make life comfy, easy and fun. Be prepared and visit your local pet-supply store before you bring your new family member home.

◆ **Collar and ID tag:** Accustom your dog to wearing a collar the first day you bring him home. Not only will a collar and ID tag help your puppy in the event that he becomes lost, but collars are also an important training tool. If your Golden gets into

trouble, the collar will act as a handle, helping you divert him to a more appropriate behavior. Make sure the collar fits snugly enough so that your retriever cannot wriggle out of it, but is loose enough so that it will not be uncomfortably tight around his neck. You should be able to fit a finger between your pup's neck and the collar. Collars come in many styles, but for starting out, a simple buckle collar with an easy-release snap works great.

◆ **Leash:** For training or just for taking a stroll down the street, a leash is your Golden's vehicle to explore the outside world. Like collars, leashes come in a variety of styles and materials. A 6-foot nylon leash is a popular choice because it is lightweight and durable. As your pup grows and gets used to walking on the leash, you may want to purchase a flexible leash. These leads allow you to extend the length to give your dog a broader area to explore or to shorten the length to keep your dog closer to you.

◆ **Bowls:** Your Golden will need two bowls: one for water and one for food. You may want two sets of bowls, one for inside and one for outside, depending on where your dog will be fed and where he will be spending time. Bowls should be sturdy enough so that they don't tip over easily. (Most have reinforced bottoms that prevent tipping.) Bowls are usually made of metal, ceramic or plastic, and should be easy to clean.

◆ **Crate:** A multipurpose crate serves as a bed, housetraining tool and travel carrier. It also is the ideal doggie den — a bedroom of sorts — that your Golden can retire to when he wants to rest or just needs a break. The crate should be large enough for your dog to stand in, turn around and lie down. You don't want any more room than this — especially if you're planning on using the crate to housetrain your dog — because he will eliminate in one corner and lie down in another.

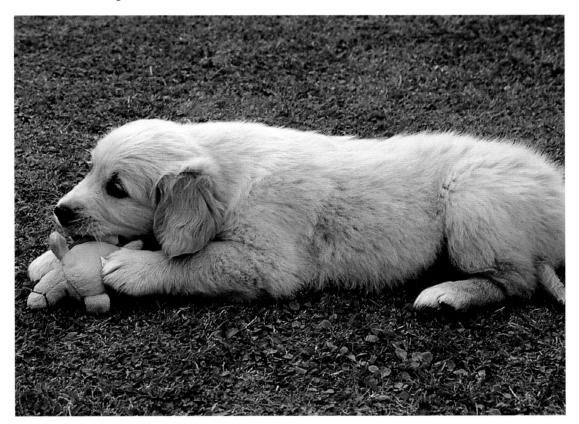

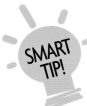

SMART TIP!

Keep a crate in your vehicle and take your Golden along when you visit the drive-thru at the bank or your favorite fast-food restaurant. She can watch interactions, hear interesting sounds and maybe even earn a dog treat.

Get a crate that is big enough for your dog when he is an adult. Then, use dividers to limit the space when he's a puppy.

◆ **Bed:** A plush doggie bed will make sleeping and resting more comfortable for your Golden. Dog beds come in all shapes, sizes and colors, but your dog just needs one that is soft and large enough for him to stretch out on. Because puppies and rescue

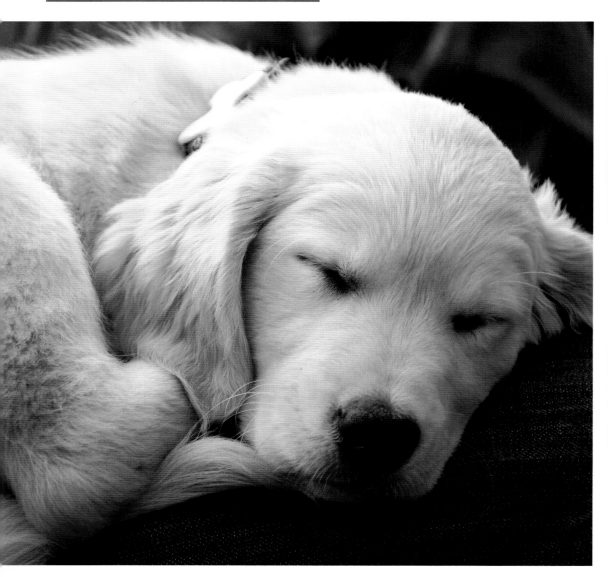

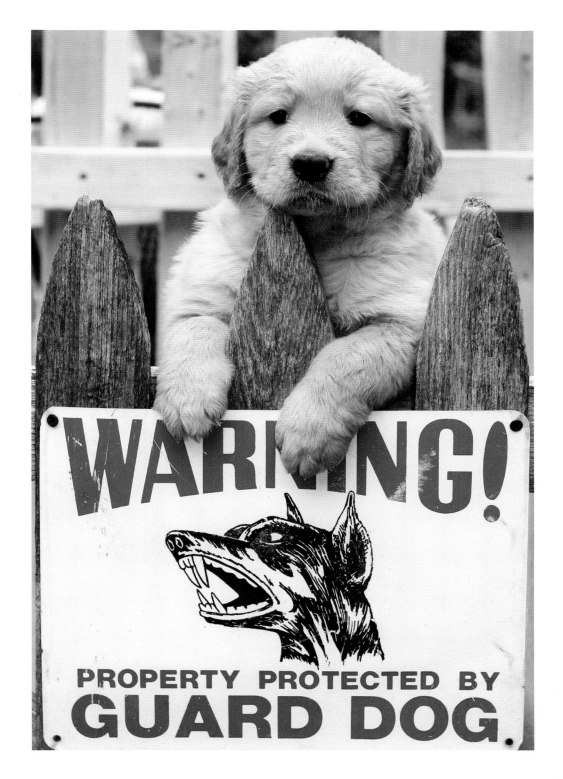

WARNING!

PROPERTY PROTECTED BY
GUARD DOG

dogs may not always be housetrained, it's helpful to buy a bed that can be easily washed. If your Golden Retriever will be sleeping in a crate, a nice crate pad and a small blanket that he can burrow in will help him feel more at home. Replace the blanket if it becomes ragged and starts to fall apart because your Golden Retriever's nails could get caught in it.

◆ **Gate:** Similar to those used for toddlers, gates help keep your Golden confined to one room or area when you can't supervise him. Gates also work to keep your dog out of areas you don't want him in. Gates are available in many styles. Make sure you choose one with openings small enough so your puppy can't squeeze through the bars or any gaps.

◆ **Toys:** Keep your dog occupied and entertained by providing him with an array of fun toys. Teething puppies like to chew — in fact, chewing is a physical need for pups as they are teething — and everything from your shoes to the leather couch to the fancy rug are fair game. Divert your Golden's

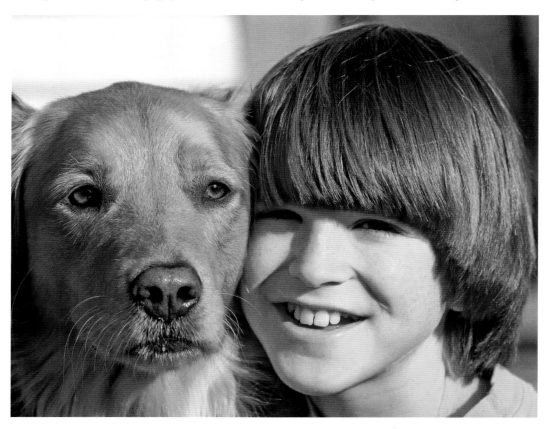

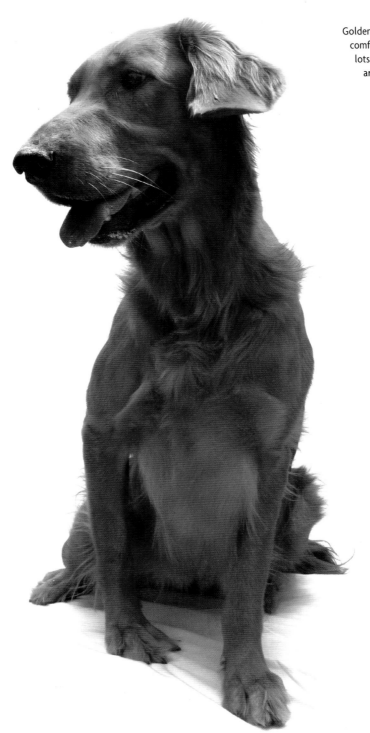

Your home is now your Golden's home, too. Make him comfortable and happy with lots of chew toys and quiet areas he can call his own.

chewing instincts with durable toys like bones made of nylon or hard rubber.

Other fun toys include rope toys, treat-dispensing toys and balls. Make sure the toys and bones don't have small parts that could break off and be swallowed, causing your dog to choke. Stuffed toys can become destuffed, and an overly excited puppy may ingest the stuffing or the squeaker. Check your Golden's toys regularly and replace them if they become frayed or show signs of wear.

◆ **Cleaning supplies:** Until your Golden Retriever puppy is housetrained, you will be doing a lot of cleaning. Accidents will occur, which is acceptable in the beginning because your puppy doesn't know any better. All you can do is be prepared to clean up any accidents. Old rags, towels, newspapers and a stain-and-odor remover are good to have on hand.

BEYOND THE BASICS

The items discussed are the bare necessities. You will find out what else your new dog will need as you go along, and these things will vary depending on your situation. It is important, that you have everything you need to make your Golden Retriever comfortable in his new home.

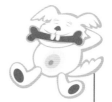

Funny Bone

To err is human; to forgive, canine.

— Anonymous

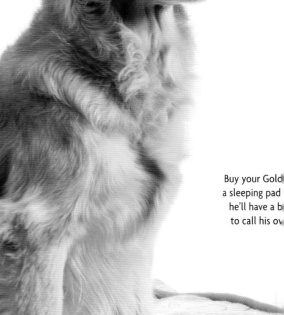

Buy your Gold[...] a sleeping pad [...] he'll have a b[...] to call his ov[...]

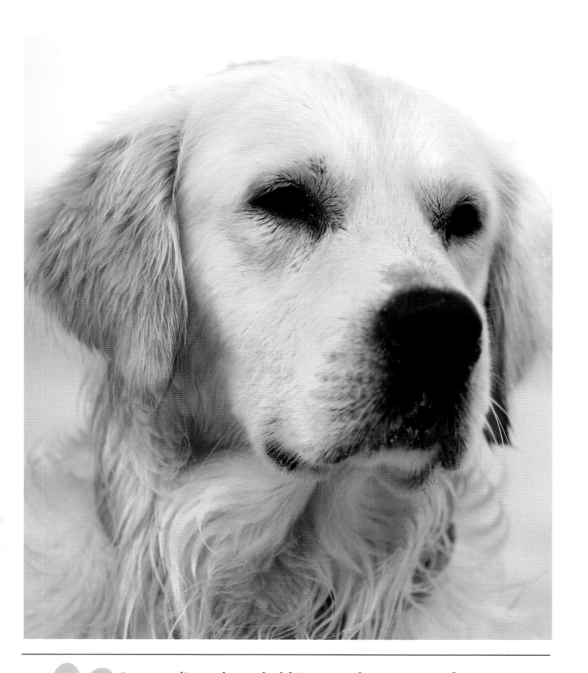

Some ordinary household items make great toys for your Golden — as long you make sure they are safe. Tennis balls, plastic water bottles, old towels and more can be transformed into fun with a little creativity. You can find a list of homemade toys at **DogChannel.com/Club-Gold**

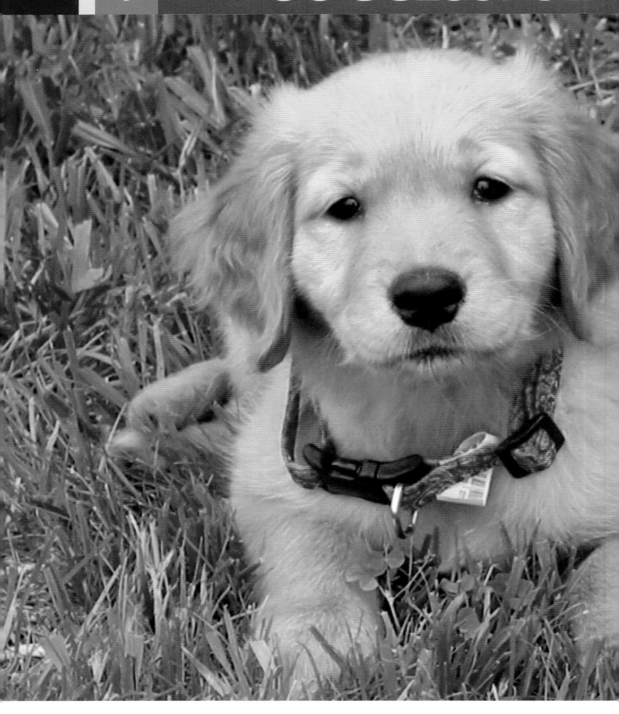

HOUSETRAINING

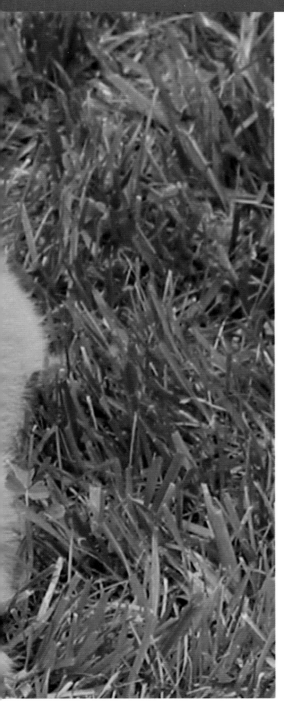

Unexciting as it may be, the housetraining part of puppy rearing greatly affects the budding relationship between a smart owner and his puppy — particularly when it becomes an area of ongoing contention. Fortunately, if you're armed with suitable knowledge, patience and common sense, housetraining will progress at a relatively smooth rate. This leaves more time for the important things, like cuddling your adorable puppy, showing him off and laughing at his high jinks.

The answer to successful housetraining is total supervision and management. This is accomplished through crates, tethers, exercise pens and leashes. Once your dog has developed preferences for outside surfaces (grass, gravel, concrete) instead of carpet, tile or hardwood, he'll understand that potty happens outside.

IN THE BEGINNING

For the first two to three weeks of a puppy's life, his mother helps the pup to eliminate. The mother also keeps the whelping box or "nest area" clean. When pups begin to walk around and eat on their

it's a Fact Ongoing housetraining difficulties may indicate your pup has a health problem, warranting a vet check. A urinary infection, parasites, a virus and other nasty issues greatly affect your puppy's ability to hold pee or poop.

own, they choose where they eliminate. You can train your puppy to relieve himself wherever you choose, but this must be somewhere suitable. Bear in mind from the outset that when your puppy is old enough to go out in public places, you must be considerate and pick up after him. You will always have to carry with you a small plastic bag or poop scoop.

Outdoor training includes surfaces such as grass, soil and concrete. Indoor training usually means training your dog on newspaper. When deciding on the surface and location that you want your Golden to use, be sure it is going to be permanent. Training your dog on grass and then changing two months later to concrete is extremely difficult for dog and owner alike.

Next, choose the cue you will use every time you want your puppy to eliminate. "Let's go," "hurry up" and "potty" are examples of cues commonly used by smart dog owners.

Use the relief cue before you take your puppy out. That way, when he becomes an adult, you will be able to determine if he wants to go out when you ask him. A confirmation from your pup will be signs of interest, such as wagging his tail, watching you intently or going to the door.

LET'S START WITH THE CRATE

Clean animals by nature, dogs dislike soiling where they sleep and eat. This fact makes a crate a useful tool for housetraining. When purchasing a new crate, consider that an appropriately sized crate will allow adequate room for an adult Golden Retriever to stand full-height, lie on his side without scrunching and turn around easily. If debating plastic versus wire crates, short-haired breeds sometimes prefer the warmer, draft-blocking quality of plastic, while furry dogs often like the cooling airflow of a wire crate.

Some crates come with a movable wall that reduces the interior size to provide enough space for your puppy to stand, turn and lie down, while not allowing him room to soil one end and sleep in the other. The problem is that if your puppy goes potty in the crate anyway, the divider forces him to lie in his own excrement.

This can work against your housetraining goals by desensitizing your puppy from his normal, instinctive revulsion to resting where he has just eliminated. If scheduling permits you or a responsible family member to clean the crate soon after it's soiled, then you can continue to crate-train because limiting crate size *does* encourage your puppy to hold it. Otherwise, give him enough room to move away from an unclean area until he's better able to control his elimination.

Needless to say, not every Golden Retriever puppy adheres to this housetraining guideline. If your Golden moves along at a faster pace, thank your lucky stars. Should he progress slower, accept it and remind yourself that he'll improve. Be aware that puppies frequently hold it longer at night than during the day. Just because your puppy sleeps for six or more hours through the night, does not mean that he can hold it that long during the more active daytime hours.

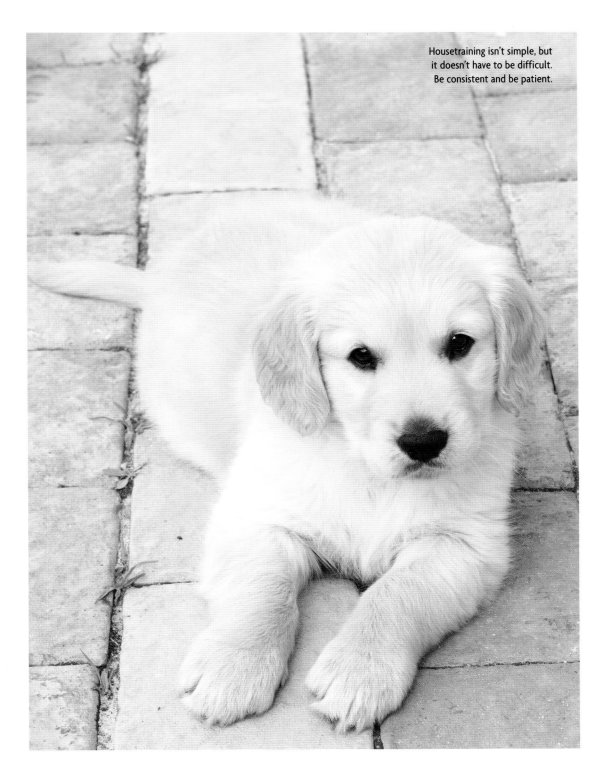

Housetraining isn't simple, but
it doesn't have to be difficult.
Be consistent and be patient.

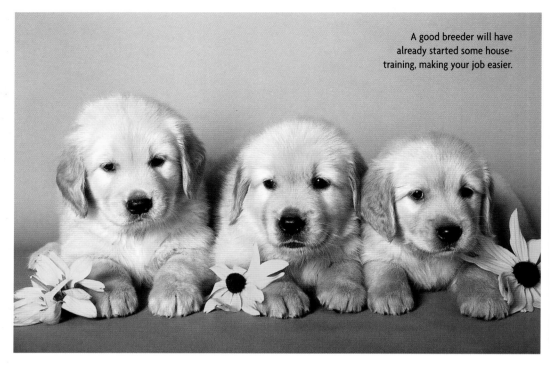

A good breeder will have already started some house-training, making your job easier.

One last bit of advice on the crate: Place it in the corner of a high-traffic room, such as the family room or kitchen. Social and curious by nature, dogs like to feel included in family happenings. Creating a quiet retreat by putting the crate in an unused area may seem like a good idea, but results in your puppy feeling insecure and isolated. Watching his people pop in and out of the crate room reassures your puppy that he's not forgotten.

A PUP'S GOT NEEDS

Your puppy needs to relieve himself after play periods, after each meal, after he has been sleeping and any time he indicates that he is looking for a place to urinate or defecate.

The urinary and intestinal tract muscles of very young puppies are not fully developed. Therefore, like human babies, puppies need to relieve themselves frequently. Take your Golden puppy out often — every hour for an 8-week-old, for example — and always immediately after sleeping and eating. The older the puppy, the less often he will need to relieve himself. Finally, as a mature, healthy adult, he will require only three to five relief trips per day.

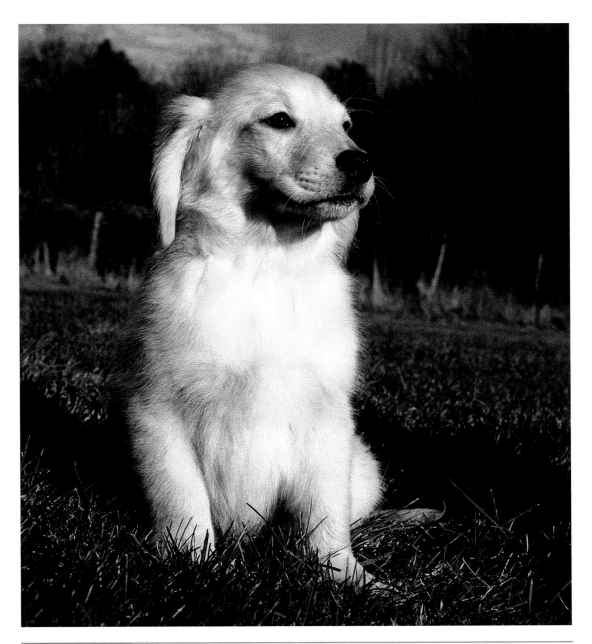

NOTABLE & QUOTABLE

Reward your pup with a high-value treat immediately after he potties to reinforce going in the proper location, then play for a short time afterward. This teaches that good things happen after pottying outside! — Victoria Schade, certified pet dog trainer, from Annandale, Va.

If you acquire your Golden puppy at 8 weeks of age, expect to take her out at least six to eight times a day. By the time she's about 6 months old, potty trips will be down to three or four times a day. A rule of thumb is to take your puppy out in hourly intervals equal to her age in months.

HOUSING HELPS

Because the types of housing and control you provide for your Golden puppy have a direct relationship on the success of housetraining, you must consider the various aspects of both before beginning training. Taking a new puppy home and turning him loose in your house can be compared to turning a child loose in a sports arena and telling the child that the place is all his! The sheer enormity of the place would be too much for him to handle. Instead, offer the puppy clearly defined areas where he can play, sleep, eat and live. A room of the house where the family gathers is the most obvious choice.

Puppies are social animals and need to feel like they are a part of the pack right from the start. Hearing your voice, watching you while you are doing things and smelling you nearby are all positive reinforcers that he is now a member of your pack. Usually a family room, the kitchen or a nearby adjoining breakfast area is ideal for providing safety and security for puppy and owner.

Within that room, there should be a smaller area that your Golden puppy can call his own. An alcove, a wire or fiberglass dog crate, or a fenced (not boarded!) corner from which he can view the activities of his new family will be fine. The designated area should be lined with clean bedding and a toy. Water must always be available, in a nonspill container, once your dog is housetrained.

IN CONTROL

By control, we mean helping the puppy to create a lifestyle pattern that will be compatible with that of his human pack (you!). Just as we guide children to learn our way of life, we must show our Golden pup when it is time to play, eat, sleep, exercise and entertain himself.

Your puppy should always sleep in his crate. He should also learn that, during times of household confusion and excessive human activity, such as at breakfast when family members are preparing for the day, he can play by himself in relative safety and comfort in his designated area. Each time you leave your Golden alone, he should understand exactly where he is supposed to stay.

Other times of excitement, such as family parties, can be fun for your puppy, provided that he can view the activities from the security of his designated area. This way he is not underfoot and is not being fed all sorts of table food that will probably cause him stomach distress, yet he still feels a part of the fun.

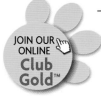

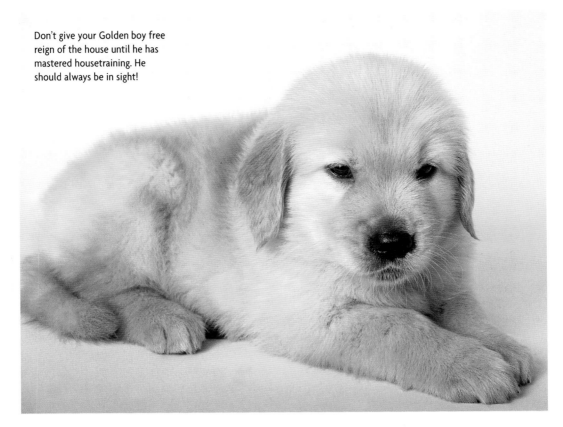

Don't give your Golden boy free reign of the house until he has mastered housetraining. He should always be in sight!

Puppies are chewers. They cannot tell the difference between lamp cords, television wires, shoes or table legs. Chewing into a television wire, for example, can be fatal to the puppy, while a shorted wire can start a fire in the house. If your puppy chews on the arm of the chair when he is alone, you probably will discipline him angrily when you get home. Thus, he makes the association that your coming home means he is going to be punished. (He will not remember chewing the chair and is incapable of making the association of the discipline with his naughty deed.)

SCHEDULE A SOLUTION

Your puppy should be taken to his relief area after meals and play sessions, and when he first awakens in the morning (at 8 weeks of age, this can mean 5 a.m.!). Your pup will indicate he's ready to go by circling or sniffing busily; do not misinterpret these signs. For a puppy less than 10 weeks of age, a routine of taking him out every hour is necessary. As your puppy grows, he will be able to wait for longer periods of time.

Did You Know?

White vinegar is a good odor remover if you don't have any professional cleaners on hand; use one-quarter cup of vinegar to one quart of water.

SMART TIP!

When proximity prevents you from going home at lunch or during periods when overtime crops up, make alternative arrangements for getting your puppy out. Hire a pet-sitting or walking service, or enlist the aid of an obliging and reliable neighbor.

Keep potty trips to your puppy's relief area short. Stay no more than 5 or 6 minutes, and then return inside. If your puppy potties during that time, lavishly praise him and then immediately take him indoors. If he does not potty, but he has an accident later when you go back indoors, pick him up, say "No!" and return to his relief area. Wait a few minutes, then return to the house again. Never hit your Golden Retriever puppy or rub his face in urine or excrement when he has had an accident.

If an accident did occur, put your puppy in his crate while you clean it up. Then release him to the family area and watch him more closely than before. Chances are, his accident was a result of your not picking up his potty signals or waiting too long before offering him the opportunity to relieve himself. Never hold a grudge against your puppy for accidents.

Let your puppy learn that going outdoors means it is time to relieve himself, not to play. Once trained, he will be able to play indoors and outdoors and still differentiate between the times for play versus the times to go potty.

Help your pup develop regular hours for naps, being alone, playing by himself and just resting — all in his crate. Encourage him to entertain himself while you are busy elsewhere. Let him learn that having you nearby is comforting, but it is not your main purpose in life to provide him with undivided attention.

Each time you put your Golden Retriever puppy in his own area, use the same command, whatever suits you best. Soon he will run to his crate or special area when he hears you say those words.

Remember, one of the primary ingredients in housetraining your puppy is control. Regardless of your lifestyle, there will always be occasions when you will need to have a place where your dog can stay and be happy and safe. Cratetraining is the answer for now and in the future.

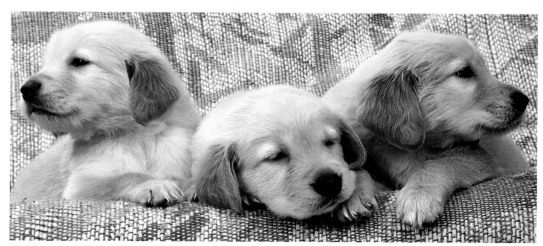

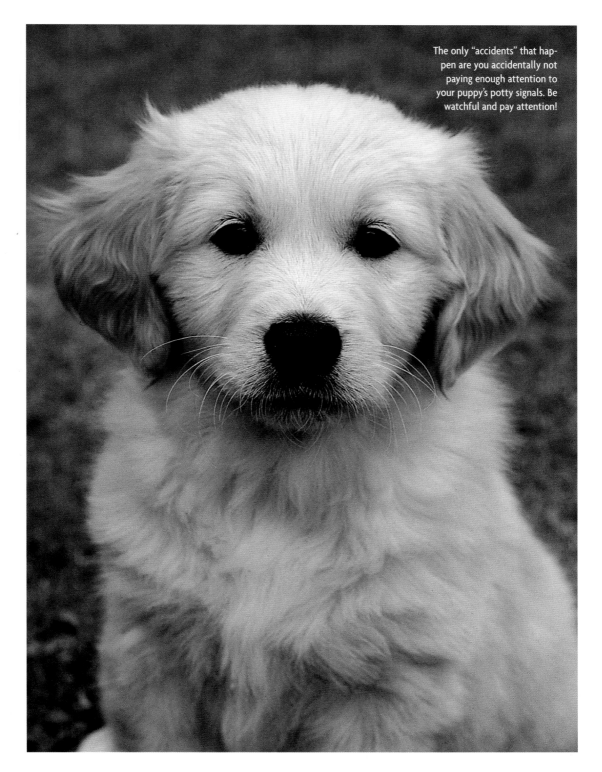

The only "accidents" that happen are you accidentally not paying enough attention to your puppy's potty signals. Be watchful and pay attention!

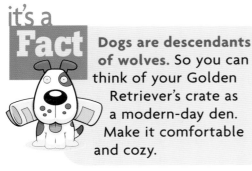

A few key elements are really all you need to implement a housetraining method that will yield successful results: consistency, frequency, praise, control and supervision. By following these procedures with a normal, healthy puppy, you and your Golden Retriever will soon be past the stage of potty accidents and ready to move on to a full and rewarding life together.

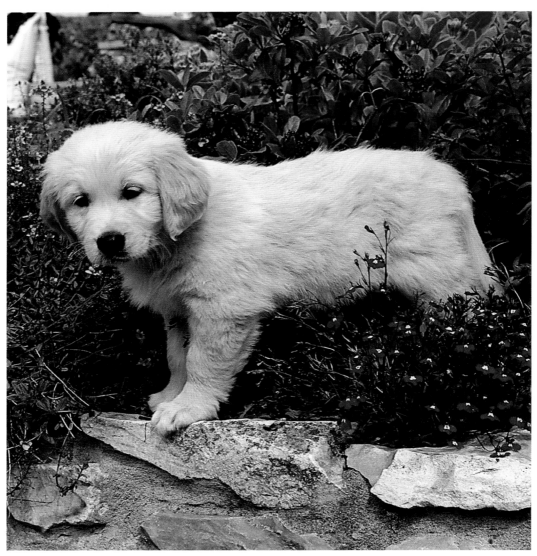

10 HOUSETRAINING HOW-TOs

1. Decide where you want your Golden Retriever to eliminate and take her there every time until she gets the idea. Pick a spot that's easy to access. Remember, puppies have very little time between "gotta go" and "oops."

2. Teach an elimination cue, such as "go potty" or "get busy." Say this every time you take your Golden to eliminate. Don't keep chanting the cue, just say it once or twice then keep quiet so you won't distract your dog.

3. Calmly praise your dog when she eliminates, but stand there a little longer in case there's more.

4. Keep potty outings for potty only. Take your dog to the designated spot, tell her "go potty" and just stand there. If she needs to eliminate, she will do so within five minutes.

5. Don't punish for potty accidents; punishment can hinder progress. If you catch your Golden in the act indoors, verbally interrupt her but don't scold. Gently carry or lead your pup to the approved spot, let her finish, then praise.

6. If it's too late to interrupt an accident, scoop the poop or blot up the urine afterward with a paper towel. Immediately take your dog and her deposit (gently!) to the potty area. Place the poop or trace of urine on the ground and praise the pup. If she sniffs at her waste, praise more. Let your Golden know you're pleased when her waste is in the proper area.

7. Keep track of when and where your Golden eliminates; this will help you anticipate potty times. Regular meals mean regular elimination, so feed your dog scheduled, measured meals instead of free-feeding (leaving food available at all times).

8. Hang a bell on a sturdy cord from the doorknob. Before you open the door to take your puppy out for potty, shake the cord and ring the bell. Most dogs soon realize the connection between the bell ringing and the door opening, then they'll try it out for themselves.

9. Dogs naturally return to re-soil where they've previously eliminated, so thoroughly clean up all accidents. Household cleaners will usually do the job, but special enzyme solutions may work better.

10. If the ground is littered with too much waste, your Golden may seek a cleaner place to eliminate. Scoop the potty area daily, leaving behind just one "reminder."

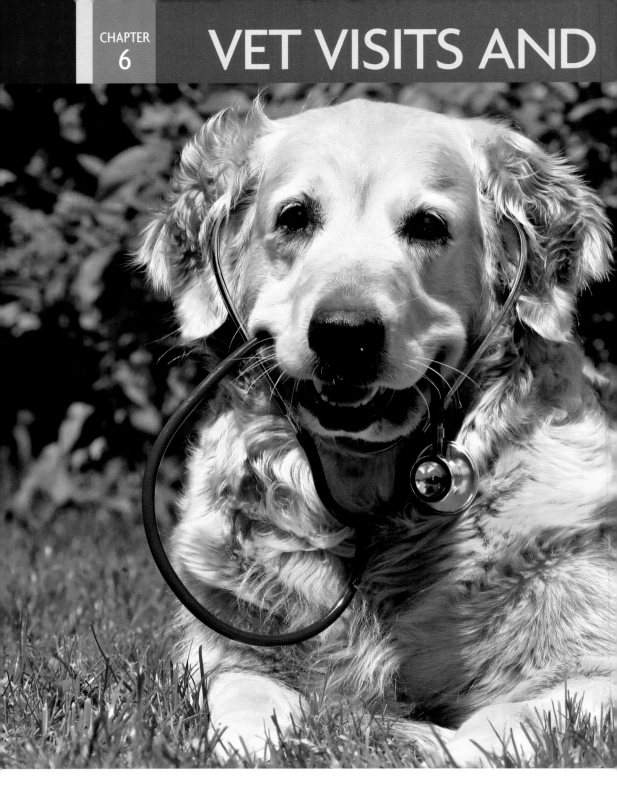

EVERYDAY CARE

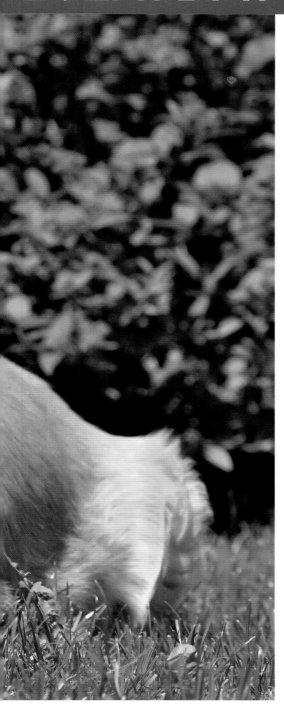

Your selection of a veterinarian for your dog should be based on personal recommendations of the doctor's skills, and, if possible, his experience with Golden Retrievers. If the veterinarian is based nearby, it will be helpful and more convenient because you might have an emergency or need to make multiple visits for treatments.

FIRST STEP: SELECT THE RIGHT VET

All licensed veterinarians are capable of dealing with routine medical issues such as infections and injuries, as well as the promotion of good health (like vaccinations). If the problem affecting your Golden is more complex, your vet may refer you to someone with more detailed knowledge of what is wrong. This usually will be a specialist such as a veterinary dermatologist or veterinary ophthalmologist.

Veterinary procedures are very costly and, as treatments improve, they are going to become more expensive. It is quite acceptable to discuss matters of cost with your vet; if there is more than one treatment option, cost may be a factor in deciding which route to take.

Smart owners will look for a veterinarian before they actually need one. For newbie pet owners, start looking for a veterinarian a month or two before you bring home your new Golden Retriever puppy. That will give you time to meet candidate veterinarians, check out the condition of the clinic, meet the staff and see who you feel most comfortable with. If you already have a Golden puppy, look sooner rather than later, preferably not in the midst of a veterinary health crisis.

Second, list the qualities that are important to you. Points to consider or investigate:

Convenience: Proximity to your home, extended hours or drop-off services are helpful for people who work regular business hours, have a busy schedule or don't want to drive far. If you have mobility issues, finding a vet who makes house calls or a service that provides pet transport might be particularly important.

Size: A one-person practice will ensure that you will always be dealing with the same vet during each and every visit. "That person can really get to know you and your dog," says Bernadine Cruz, D.V.M., of Laguna Hills Animal Hospital in Laguna Hills, Calif. The downside is that the sole practitioner does not have the immediate input of another vet, and if your vet becomes ill or takes time off, you are out of luck.

A multiple-doctor practice offers consistency if your dog needs to come in unexpectedly on a day when your veterinarian isn't there. Additionally, your vet can quickly consult with his colleagues within the clinic if he's unsure about a diagnosis or a treatment.

If you find a veterinarian within that practice who you really like, you can make your appointments with that individual, establishing the same kind of bond that you would with the solo practitioner.

Appointment Policies: Some practices are by-appointment only, which could minimize your wait time. However, if a sudden problem arises with your Golden and the veterinarians are booked up, they might not be able to squeeze your pet in that day. Some clinics are walk-in only, which is great for impromptu or crisis visits, but without scheduling may involve longer waits to see the next available veterinarian. Some practices offer the best of both worlds by maintaining an appointment schedule but also keeping slots open throughout the day for walk-ins.

Basic vs. Full Service vs. State-of-the-Art: A veterinarian practice with high-tech equipment offers greater diagnostic capabilities and treatment options, important for tricky or difficult cases. However, pricey equipment costs are passed along to the client, so you could pay more for routine procedures — the bulk of most pets' appointments. Some practices offer boarding,

---

Picking the right vet is one of the most important decisions you'll make for the lifelong health of your new family member. Make sure you ask the right questions to ensure that your vet is knowledgeable not only about dogs, but also about Golden Retrievers in particular. Download a list of questions to ask potential vets by logging on to **DogChannel.com/Club-Gold** — just click on "Downloads."

JOIN OUR ONLINE
Club Gold™

grooming, training classes and other services on the premises — conveniences some pet owners appreciate.

Fees and Payment Polices: How much is a routine visit? If there is a significant price difference, ask why. If you intend to carry health insurance on your Golden or want to pay by credit card, check that the clinic accepts those payment options.

FIRST VET VISIT

It is much easier, less costly and more effective to practice preventive medicine than to fight bouts of illness and disease. Properly bred puppies of all breeds come from parents who were selected based upon their genetic disease profile. The puppies' mother should have been vaccinated, free of all internal and external parasites, and properly nourished. For these reasons, a visit to the veterinarian who

cared for the mother is recommended if at all possible. The mother passes disease resistance to her puppies, which should last from 8 to 10 weeks. Unfortunately, she also can pass on parasites and infection.

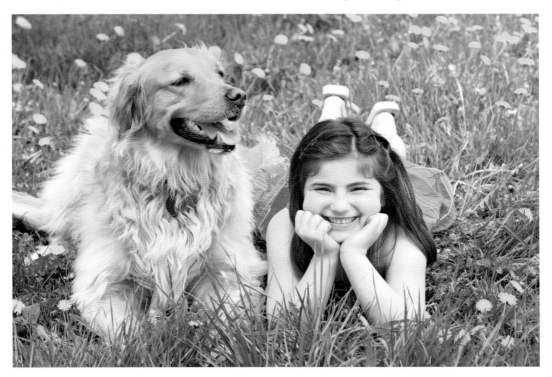

This is why knowing about her health is useful in learning more about the health of her puppies.

Now that you have your Golden puppy home safe and sound, it's time to arrange your pup's first trip to the veterinarian. Perhaps the breeder can recommend someone in the area who specializes in Golden Retrievers, or maybe you know other Golden owners who can suggest a good vet. Either way, you should make an appointment within a couple of days of bringing home your puppy. If possible, see if you can stop for this first vet appointment before going home.

The pup's first vet visit will consist of an overall examination to make sure that your pup does not have any problems that are not apparent to you. The veterinarian will also set up a schedule for the pup's vaccinations; the breeder should inform you of which ones your puppy has already received, and the vet can continue from there.

Your puppy also will have his teeth examined and have his skeletal conformation and general health checked prior to certification by the veterinarian. Puppies in certain breeds have problems with their kneecaps, cataracts and other eye problems, heart murmurs and undescended testicles. They may also have behavioral problems, which your veterinarian can evaluate if he or she has had relevant training.

VACCINATION SCHEDULING

Most vaccinations are given by injection and should only be given by a veterinarian. Both you and the vet should keep a record of the date of the injection, the identification of the vaccine and the amount given. Some vets give a first vaccination at 8 weeks of age, but most dog breeders prefer the course not commence until about 10 weeks because of interaction with the antibodies produced by the mother. The vaccination scheduling is usually based on a 15-day cycle. You must take your vet's advice as to when to vaccinate, as this may differ according to the vaccine used.

The usual vaccines contain immunizing doses of several different viruses such as distemper, parvovirus, parainfluenza and hepatitis. There are other vaccines available when the puppy is at a greater risk for viral exposures. You should rely on your vet's advice. This is especially true for the booster

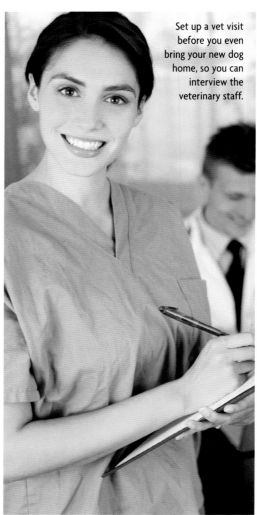

Set up a vet visit before you even bring your new dog home, so you can interview the veterinary staff.

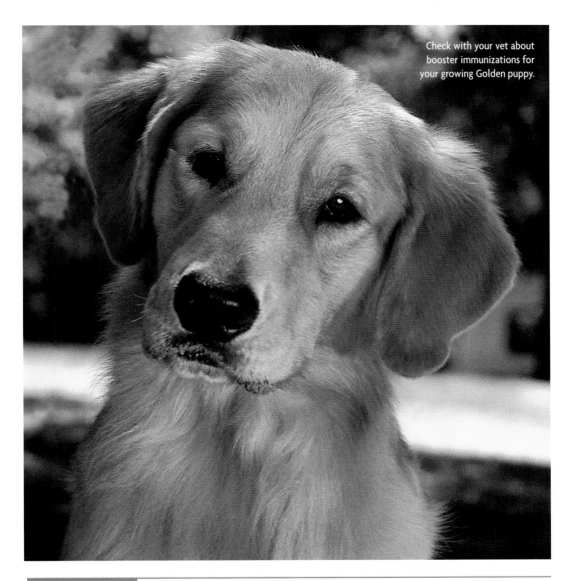

Check with your vet about booster immunizations for your growing Golden puppy.

NOTABLE & QUOTABLE

A dog with a mild case of subvalvular aortic stenosis might live his whole life and never show any clinical signs. Moderately affected dogs may or may not exhibit some symptoms including exercise intolerance or collapse. Severely affected dogs tend to show these symptoms or succumb to sudden cardiac death within the first couple of years of life. — William Rausch, D.V.M., of the Oregon Veterinary Referral Associates in Springfield, Ore.

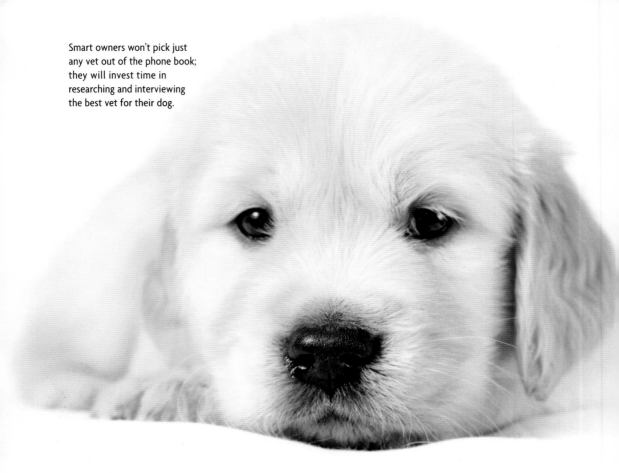

immunizations. Most vaccination programs require a booster when the puppy is a year old and once a year thereafter. In some cases, circumstances may require more frequent immunizations.

Kennel cough, more formally known as *tracheobronchitis*, is combatted with a vaccine that is sprayed into the dog's nostrils. Kennel cough is usually included in routine vaccinations, but it is often not as effective as the vaccines for other major diseases.

Your veterinarian probably will recommend that your Golden Retriever puppy be fully vaccinated before you take him on outings. Airborne diseases, parasite eggs in the grass and unexpected visits from other dogs might be dangerous to your puppy's health. Other dogs are the most harmful reservoir of pathogenic organisms, as everything they have can be transmitted to your puppy.

6 Months to 1 Year of Age: Unless you intend to breed or show your dog, neutering or spaying your Golden at 6 months of age is recommended. Discuss this with your veterinarian. Neutering and spaying have proven to be beneficial to male and female puppies, respectively. Besides eliminating the possibility of pregnancy, it inhibits (but does not prevent) breast cancer in females and prostate cancer in male dogs.

Your veterinarian should provide your Golden puppy with a thorough dental evaluation at 6 months of age, ascertaining

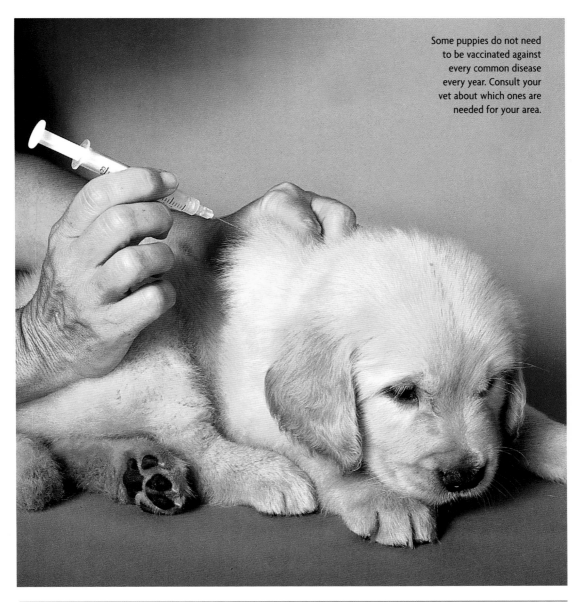

Some puppies do not need to be vaccinated against every common disease every year. Consult your vet about which ones are needed for your area.

Many dogs have incipient [tiny and immature] cataracts. These do not significantly impair vision, so the dog can lead a normal life with close to normal vision. However, some cataracts become larger and mature [until] they fill the entire lens, completely obstructing the dog's vision. — Dan Lorimer, D.V.M., founder and head of *ophthalmology at Michigan Veterinary Specialists*

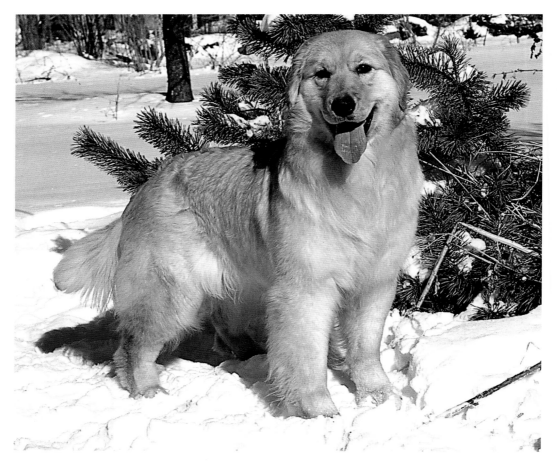

whether all his permanent teeth have erupted properly. A home dental care regimen should be initiated at 6 months, including weekly brushing and providing good dental devices (such as nylon bones). Regular dental care promotes healthy teeth, fresh breath and a longer life.

Dogs Older Than 1 Year: Continue to visit the veterinarian at least once a year as bodily functions do change with age. The eyes and ears are no longer as efficient; liver, kidney and intestinal functions often decline. Proper dietary changes recommended by your veterinarian can make life more pleasant for your aging Golden and you.

EVERYDAY HAPPENINGS

Keeping your Golden Retriever healthy is a matter of keen observation and quick action when necessary. Knowing what is normal for your dog will help you to recognize signs of trouble before they blossom into a full-blown emergency situation. Even if the problem is minor, such as a cut or scrape, you will want to care for it immediately to prevent infection, as well as to ensure that your dog doesn't make it worse by chewing or scratching at it. Here's what to do for common, minor injuries or illnesses, and how to recognize and deal with emergencies.

Cuts and Scrapes: For a cut or scrape that's half an inch or smaller, clean the

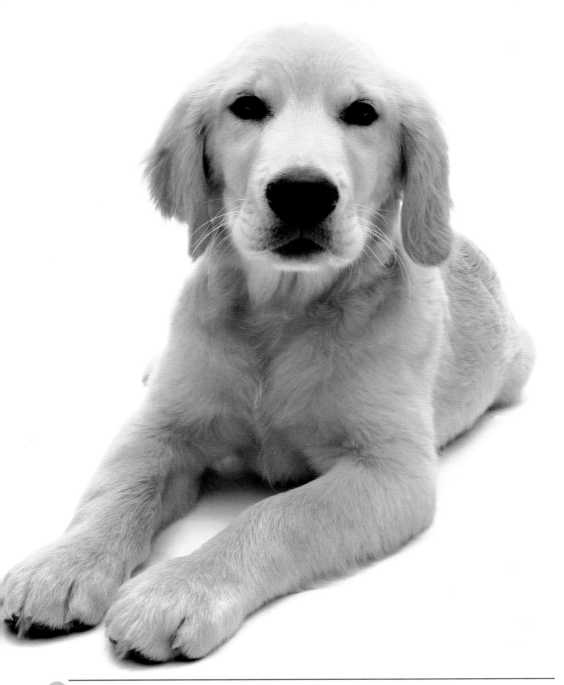

Just like with infants, puppies need a series of vaccinations to ensure that they stay healthy during their first year of life. Download a vaccination chart from **DogChannel.com/Club-Gold** that you can fill out for your Golden Retriever.

wound with saline solution or warm water and use tweezers to remove any splinters or other debris. Apply an antibiotic ointment. No bandage is necessary unless the wound is on a paw, which can pick up dirt when your dog walks on it. Deep cuts with lots of bleeding or those caused by glass or some other object should be treated by your veterinarian.

Cold Symptoms: Dogs do not actually get colds, but they can get illnesses that have similar symptoms, such as coughing, a runny nose or sneezing. Your Golden may cough for any number of reasons, from respiratory infections to inhaled irritants to congestive heart failure. Take your Golden Retriever to the veterinarian for prolonged coughing, or coughing accompanied by labored breathing, runny eyes and nose, or bloody phlegm.

A runny nose that continues for more than several hours requires veterinary attention. If your Golden Retriever sneezes, he may have some mild nasal irritation that will resolve on its own, but frequent sneezing, especially if it's accompanied by a runny nose, may indicate anything from allergies to an infection or something stuck in his nose.

Vomiting and Diarrhea: Sometimes dogs can suffer minor gastric upset when they eat a new type of food, eat too much, eat the contents of the trash can or become excited or anxious. If that happens to your Golden, give his stomach a rest by withholding food for 12 hours, and then feeding him a bland diet such as rice and chicken, gradually returning your dog to his normal food. Projectile vomiting or vomiting or diarrhea that continues for more than 48 hours, is another matter. If this happens, immediately take your Golden Retriever to the veterinarian.

MORE HEALTH HINTS

A Golden Retriever's anal glands can cause problems if not periodically evacuated. In the wild, dogs regularly clear their anal glands to mark their territory. In domestic dogs this function is no longer necessary; thus, their contents can build up and clog, causing discomfort. Signs that the anal glands — located on both sides of the anus — need emptying are if a Golden drags his rear end along the ground or keeps turning around to lick the area of discomfort.

While care must be taken not to cause injury, anal glands can be evacuated by pressing gently on either side of the anal opening and by using a piece of cotton or a tissue to collect the foul-smelling matter. If anal glands are allowed to become impacted, abscesses can form, causing pain and the need for veterinary attention.

Goldens can get into all sorts of mischief, so it is not uncommon for them to swallow something poisonous in the course of their investigations. Obviously, an urgent visit to the vet is required under such circumstances, but if possible, when you call your vet, inform him which poisonous substance has been ingested, because different treatments are needed. Should it be necessary to cause your dog to vomit (which is not always the case with poisoning), a small lump of baking soda, given orally, will have an immediate effect. Alternatively, a small teaspoon of salt or mustard, dissolved in water, will have a similar effect but may be more difficult to administer and take longer to work.

Golden puppies often have painful fits while they are teething. These are not usually serious and are brief. Of course, you must be certain that the cause is nothing more than teething. Giving a puppy something hard to chew on usually will solve this temporary problem.

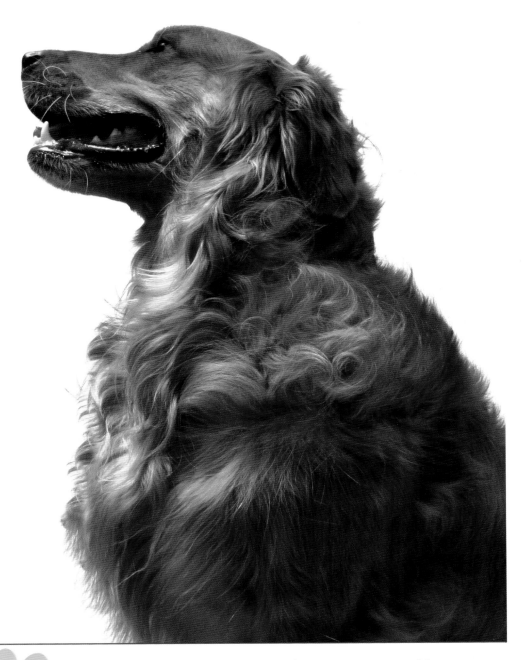

No matter how careful you are with your precious Golden, some-times unexpected injuries happen. Be prepared for an emergency by creating a canine first-aid kit. Find out what essentials you need on **DogChannel.com/Club-Gold** — just click on "Downloads."

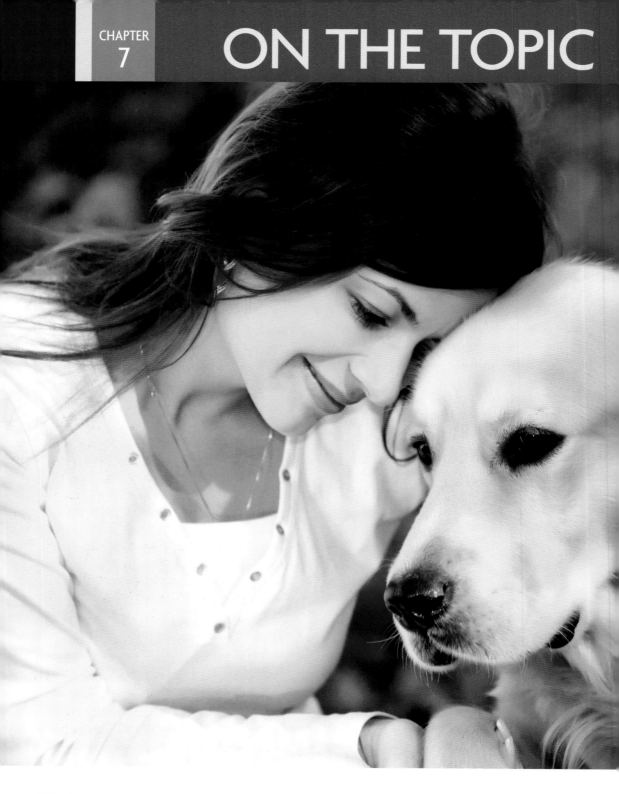

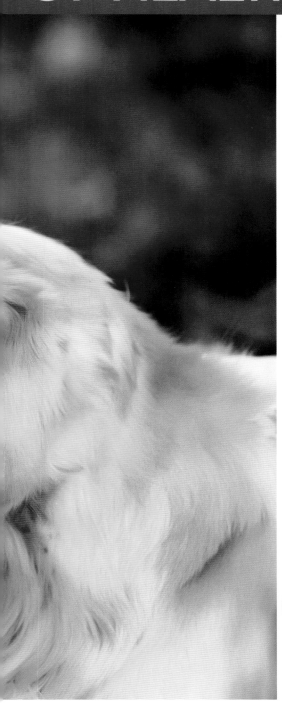

If extraterrestrials landed on Earth and wanted to meet representatives from every species, surely the Golden Retriever would serve as the canine ambassador, for what breed could better represent all that is good in a dog?

The Golden Retriever is loving, easygoing, playful and eager to please. Their enthusiasm and easy trainability allow them to excel in a variety of roles: therapy, service, guide, drug detection and search-and-rescue work; retrieving, obedience, agility, Frisbee and flyball competitions; and most of all, as an excellent friend and family member. It's no wonder the Golden is among America's favorite dogs.

However, the Golden Retriever's immense popularity has not always served the breed well. The casual breeding practices of unethical breeders have contributed to some of the hereditary problems that trouble today's Golden Retriever. Cataracts, hip dysplasia and a form of heart disease known as subvalvular aortic stenosis rank high on the Golden's list of genetic problems.

Despite the serious nature of these health problems, the Golden Retriever is not alone in carrying genetic diseases. All animals, including random-bred dogs, cats and human beings, carry defective genes

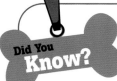

Did You Know?

Dogs can get many diseases from ticks, including Lyme disease, Rocky Mountain spotted fever, tick bite paralysis and many others.

that cause hereditary disease. Fortunately for Golden Retriever lovers, conscientious breeders and dedicated veterinary researchers are using the tools available to them to minimize and perhaps someday eliminate the most persistent or serious inherited diseases.

CHRONIC HIP DYSPLASIA

Chronic hip dysplasia results in a loose hip joint and abnormal rubbing of the joint surfaces. The joint eventually becomes inflamed, causing chronic pain and even the development of arthritis. The most common heritable orthopedic disease in dogs, chronic hip dysplasia is also the No. 1 genetic health problem seen in dogs, and the Golden Retriever is no exception.

Clinical signs of hip dysplasia include limping, difficulty getting up, stiffness, altered gait, struggling to go up stairs or get into the car and reduced interest in play. Treatment options vary depending upon the type of symptoms your dog experiences, his age and when he is diagnosed. Conservative treatments for mildly dysplastic dogs include:

Golden Retrievers are a healthy breed, but genetic problems can crop up in any breed.

- weight control. Shedding extra pounds is often enough to decrease or eliminate joint pain in dogs.
- prescription diets to help improve joint function. Choose a formula that contains omega-3 fatty acids for best results. Some of these formulas also contain glucosamine and chondroitin, although the amounts may not be adequate, according to Darryl Millis, D.V.M., who is also a professor of orthopedic surgery at the University of Tennessee, Knoxville. "These diets replace the need for separate supplementation with omega-3 fatty acids," Millis says.
- glucosamine/chondroitin supplements to promote joint health (if not provided in adequate amounts in your Golden Retriever's food). Studies in arthritic humans found that glucosamine/chondroitin supplements helped those with moderate to severe knee pain. However, well-controlled, long-term studies are still needed in clinically affected animals.
- pain-relief drugs (anti-inflammatories prescribed under veterinary

supervision). Some dogs show better results with one medication over another, so you may have to try a couple of different types before finding one that works best for your dog.

● regular exercise to maintain muscle tone, strength and range of motion in the joint. Regular, low-impact activity such as swimming or leash walks at a speed and distance your dog can handle (not to the point of lameness or stiffness) are recommended. Another good exercise is "dancing" the dog forward. "Pick up the dog's forelimbs and walk him forward as you walk backward," Millis explains. "This strengthens the gluteal muscles and helps reduce arthritis pain. But don't walk the dog backward, as this could cause hip pain because of the more extended position of the hip joint."

● TENS (transcutaneous electrical nerve stimulation), a device that uses electrical impulse to reduce pain. "We found positive response to that," Millis says. "Most treatments last 20 to 30 minutes."

● ESWT (extracorporeal shockwave therapy), a treatment that uses sound waves to induce pain relief. "We tested dogs who were pretty bad and found, in general, a single treatment lasted several months," Millis says. Studies elsewhere found that less severely affected dogs achieved pain relief for up to two years.

More severely affected dogs as well as young dogs may best be served by surgical procedures. Surgical options include:

▲ JPS (juvenile pubic symphysidesis). If diagnosed before a puppy reaches 14 to 16 weeks of age, this simple, minimally invasive procedure can be performed, often in combination with an early spay or neuter. With this procedure, growing cartilage cells in the lower pelvis are cauterized to create a tighter hip joint. "Most puppies aren't symptomatic by that age," Millis notes, "but for high-risk

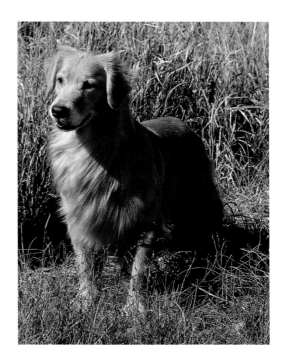

dogs or loose-hipped puppies, it may be beneficial to perform JPS prophylactically during a spay or neuter."

▲ TPO (triple pelvic osteotomy). The pelvic bone is cut in three places and repositioned to better secure the hip femoral head. "TPO is best performed in growing dogs with minimal or no arthritic changes," Millis states. "It doesn't work as well after arthritic changes have occurred. That's a mistake some dog owners make: They adopt a wait-and-see attitude and in as little as two to four weeks, they lose their window of opportunity for that procedure."

▲ femoral head and neck incision. Best for dogs weighing less than 50 pounds, this technique removes the femoral head and neck, forming a false joint.

▲ hip replacement surgery. Although expensive, hip replacement surgery provides your dog with a functional, albeit artificial, hip. "Many dogs with a hip replacement have a profound improvement in their quality of their life," Millis reports.

Prognosis varies, depending upon treatment options and the severity of the disease. Mildly affected dogs can often be successfully managed with conservative treatments for a long time. The outlook for hip repair and reconstruction generally ranges from good to excellent.

Although hip dysplasia is a genetic disorder, other causes include overfeeding and over- or under-supplementation of carbohydrates, calcium and phosphorous in growing dogs. Talk with your vet to find the appropriate diet formula for your dog.

CATARACTS

Cataract is a condition in which part or all of an eye's lens becomes opaque. Depending upon the severity, the opacity may be slight, appearing as white flecks in the eye and never interfering with the dog's vision. Or, it may progress into a more solid-looking, milky-gray cast that covers much of the eye, resulting in severe or total vision loss.

Some of the many causes of cataracts include genetic disease, diabetes and trauma.

SMART TIP! Many canine skin irritations can be reduced or simply avoided by employing a simple preventive regimen.

- Keep your Golden Retriever's skin clean and dry.
- Shampoo your dog regularly (especially during allergy season) with a hypoallergenic shampoo.
- Rinse the coat thoroughly.
- Practice good flea control.
- Supplement your dog's diet with fatty acids, such as omega-3.

Clinical signs are varied. "If the lens is completely cataractous, then the eye looks milky-white, and the dog has severe visual problems," says Gregory M. Acland, B.V.S.c., Diplomate American College of Veterinary Ophthalmology. "But many cataracts never reach that state, so visual impairment may be fairly subtle or even nonexistent."

Diagnosis is made by dilating the eye and examining it with magnification and a strong light source. Although mature or complete cataracts can be recognized by a general veterinarian, small cataracts can be found only by using the high-tech equipment usually found in a veterinary ophthalmology practice.

The sole treatment is surgical removal of the cataract. "If undertaken by a surgeon who's well-trained in microsurgery and has the appropriate instrumentation, the surgery has a very high success rate," Acland says.

In the Golden Retriever, hereditary cataracts usually show up under examination by 18 months of age. It's important, emphasizes Acland, that breeders begin having their dogs' eyes examined at a young age. "Some cataracts start quite young and are extremely characteristic [of their type, e.g. genetic] when they start," he says. "In later life, if they progress, you can't always tell if it's a genetic cataract or some other form." In order to make more well-informed breeding program decisions, it is important to know if cataracts in breeding prospects are hereditary or nonhereditary.

SUBVALVULAR AORTIC STENOSIS

Subvalvular aortic stenosis, also known as subaortic stenosis or SAS, is a form of congenital heart disease. According to a nationwide survey conducted by Dr. James Buchanen at the University of Pennsylvania, SAS is the second most common congenital heart disease seen in general veterinary practices. At the university's veterinary hospital, it is the most prevalent congenital cardiac defect seen, which probably mirrors the incidence at most veterinary cardiology practices. An odds ratio from Buchanen's study found that Golden Retrievers ranked as the second highest breed at risk for SAS, being 7.2 times more likely to have the disease than some mixed-breed dogs.

SAS is usually first detected in puppyhood when the veterinarian hears a heart murmur over the aortic valve. Because the disease may be progressive early in life, a murmur may be easier to detect in a 16-week-old puppy than in an 8-week-old puppy. Additionally, young puppies can have innocent murmurs — those not caused by a heart defect — that disappear by 16 weeks of age, making the ideal time for SAS screening around 16 weeks.

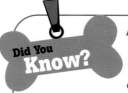

Did You Know? Across the globe, more than 800 species of ticks exist, and they aren't particular to where they dine. Mammals, birds and reptiles are all fair game.

In an affected dog, a ridge of abnormal tissue develops, creating an obstruction or narrowing of the blood flow just below the aortic valve. As in a pinched garden hose, in which water dams up behind the narrowed area, the obstruction in the heart causes pressure to build up behind the narrowing. The ventricle then has to work harder to pump against and over the obstruction. As a result, the left ventricle becomes very thick and could use more blood than what's supplied, causing irregular heart rhythms to develop. The end result is an affected dog who seems completely normal will die suddenly.

The prognosis varies with the severity of the disease. "Mildly affected dogs, with some exceptions, have a normal life span," says Linda Lehmkuhl, D.V.M., M.S., Diplomate American College of Veterinary Internal Medicine. "They are at very little risk for complications. They can be athletic, do whatever they want to and live to die from some other disease.

"A dog that is moderately or severely affected is at pretty high risk for sudden death, usually associated with a cardiac arrhythmia [irregular heartbeat]," Lehmkuhl continues. "Another complication they can develop is left-sided congestive heart failure. Many severely affected dogs die before 3 years of age."

This is good news for mildly affected

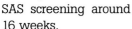

dogs, but it's less hopeful for moderately to severely affected dogs. "The heart is working hard every day because of this obstruction, and over time that overworked heart becomes a problem," Lehmkuhl explains. "Commonly, a dog can be asymptomatic, have no clinical signs and feel great until it's 18 months, then drop dead. Did it drop dead because the ridge got worse between 12 and 18 months? Unlikely. The dog died because the disease that it had for 18 months took its toll."

Treatment options consist of surgery, balloon dilation and medical therapy. The long-term effects of these treatments are unknown. Surgical removal of the obstruction can help the most, Lehmkuhl says. "You can decrease the severity of the disease the most if you go in, open the chest and cut out the ridge." However, she warns, the mortality rate is high, the cost is expensive and very few places have access to a cardiopulmonary bypass machine and a team experienced in this procedure.

OTHER HEALTH CONCERNS

Airborne allergies: Just as humans suffer from hay fever during allergy season, many dogs suffer from the same. When the pollen count is high, your Golden might suffer, but don't expect him to sneeze or have a runny nose like a human. Goldens react to pollen allergies in the same way they react to fleas; they scratch and bite themselves. Dogs, like humans, can be tested for allergens. Be sure to discuss allergy testing with your vet.

Autoimmune illness: An autoimmune illness is one in which the immune system overacts and does not recognize parts of the affected person. Instead, the immune system starts to react as if these parts were foreign cells and need to be destroyed. An example of an autoimmune illness is rheumatoid arthritis, which occurs when the body does not recognize the joints. This leads to a very painful and damaging reaction in the joints. Rheumatoid arthritis has nothing to do with age, so it can also occur in puppies. The wear-and-tear arthritis in older people or dogs is called osteoarthritis.

Lupus is another autoimmune disease that affects dogs as well as people. It can take variable forms, affecting the kidneys, bones and skin. It can be fatal, so it is treated with steroids, which have very significant side effects. Steroids calm down the allergic reaction to the body's tissues, which helps the lupus, but also affects the

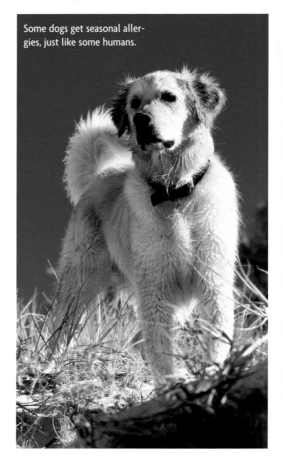

Some dogs get seasonal allergies, just like some humans.

body's reaction to actual foreign cells such as bacteria; they also thin the skin and bones.

Food Allergies: Properly feeding your Golden is very important. An incorrect diet could affect your dog's health, behavior and nervous system, possibly making a normal dog aggressive. The result of a good or bad diet is most visible in a dog's skin and coat, but internal organs are affected, too.

Dogs are allergic to many foods that are popular and highly recommended by breeders and veterinarians. Changing the brand of food may not eliminate the problem if the ingredient to which your dog is allergic is contained in the new brand.

Recognizing a food allergy can be difficult. Humans often have rashes or swelling of the lips or eyes when they eat foods they are allergic to. Dogs do not usually develop rashes, but they react the same way they do to an airborne allergy or parasite bite; they itch, scratch and bite. While pollen allergies and parasite bites are usually seasonal, food allergies are year-round problems.

Diagnosis of a food allergy is based on a two- to four-week dietary trial with a home-cooked diet, excluding all other foods. The diet should consist of boiled rice or potato with a source of protein that your Golden has never eaten before, such as fresh or frozen fish, lamb or even something as exotic as pheasant. Water has to be the only drink, and it is important that no other foods are fed during this trial. If your dog's condition improves, try the original diet again to see if the itching resumes. If it does, then your dog is allergic to his original diet. You must find a diet that does not stress your dog's skin. Start with a commercially available hypoallergenic food or the homemade diet that you created for the allergy trial.

SMART TIP!

Brush your dog's teeth every day. Plaque colonizes on the tooth surface in as little as six to eight hours, and if not removed by brushing, forms calculus (tartar) within three to five days. Plaque and tartar cause gum disease, periodontal disease, loosening of the teeth and tooth loss. In bad cases of dental disease, bacteria from the mouth can get into the bloodstream, leading to kidney or heart problems — all of which are life-shortening.

Food intolerance is the inability to completely digest certain foods. This occurs because the dog does not have the enzymes necessary to digest some foodstuffs. All puppies have the enzymes needed to digest canine milk, but some dogs do not have the enzymes to digest cow milk, resulting in loose bowels, stomach pains and flatulence.

Dogs often do not have the enzymes to digest soy or other beans. The treatment is to exclude these foods from your Golden's diet.

EXTERNAL PARASITES

Insect bites itch, erupt and can become infected. Dogs have essentially the same reaction to fleas, ticks and mites. When an insect lands on you, you can whisk it away. Unfortunately, when your Golden is bitten by a flea, tick or mite, he can only scratch or bite.

By the time your Golden has been bitten, the parasite has done its damage. It also may have laid eggs, which will cause further problems. The itching from parasite bites is probably due to the saliva injected into the site when the parasite sucks the dog's blood.

Fleas: Of all the health and grooming problems to which canines are susceptible, none is better known and more frustrating than fleas. Flea infestation is relatively simple to cure but difficult to prevent.

To control flea infestation, you have to understand the flea's life cycle. Fleas are often thought of as a summertime problem, but centrally heated homes have made fleas a year-round problem. The most effective method of flea control is a two-stage approach: kill the adult fleas, then control the development of pupae (pre-adult) fleas. Unfortunately, no single active ingredient is effective against all stages of the flea life cycle.

Treating fleas should be a two-pronged attack. First, the environment needs to be treated; this includes carpets and furniture, especially your Golden's bedding and areas underneath furniture. The environment should be treated with a household spray containing an insect growth regulator and an insecticide to kill adult fleas. Most insecticides are effective against eggs and larvae; they actually mimic the fleas' own hormones and stop the eggs and larvae from developing into adult fleas. There are currently no treatments available to attack the pupae stage of the life cycle, so the adult insecticide is used to kill the newly hatched adult fleas before they find a host. Most insect growth regulators are active for many months, while adult insecticides are only active for a few days.

When treating fleas with a household spray, vacuum before applying the product. This stimulates as many pupae as possible to hatch into adult fleas. The vacuum cleaner should also be treated with an insecticide to prevent the eggs and larvae that have been collected in the vacuum bag from hatching.

The second stage of treatment is to apply an adult insecticide to your Golden Retriever. Traditionally, this would be in the form of a collar or a spray, but more recent innovations include digestible insecticides that poison the fleas when they ingest the dog's blood. Alternatively, there are drops that, when placed on the back of the dog's neck, spread throughout the hair and skin to kill adult fleas.

Ticks: Though not as common as fleas, ticks are found all over the tropical and temperate world. They don't bite like fleas; they harpoon. They dig their sharp *proboscis* (nose) into your Golden Retriever's skin and drink the blood, which is their only food and drink. Ticks are controlled the same way fleas are controlled.

The American dog tick, *Dermacentor variabilis*, may be the most common dog tick in many areas, especially those areas where the climate is hot and humid. Most dog ticks have life expectancies of a week to 6 months, depending on climatic conditions. They can neither jump nor fly, but they can crawl slowly and can travel up to 16 feet to reach a sleeping or unsuspecting dog.

Mites: Just as fleas and ticks can be problematic for your dog, mites can also lead to an itch fit. Microscopic in size, mites are related to ticks and generally take up permanent residence on their host animal — in this case, your Golden. The term "mange" refers to any infestation caused by one of the mighty mites, of which there are six varieties that smart dog owners should know about.

■ Demodex mites cause a condition known as *demodicosis* (sometimes called "red mange" or "follicular mange"), in which the mites live in the dog's hair follicles and sebaceous glands in larger-than-normal numbers. Most dogs recover from this type of mange without any treatment, though topical therapies are commonly prescribed by the veterinarian.

■ The *Cheyletiellosis* mite is the hook-mouthed culprit associated with "walking dandruff," a condition that affects dogs as well as cats and rabbits. If untreated, this mange can affect a whole kennel of dogs and can be spread to humans as well.

■ The *Sarcoptes* mite causes intense itching on the dog in the form of a condition known as scabies or sarcoptic mange. Scabies is highly contagious and can be

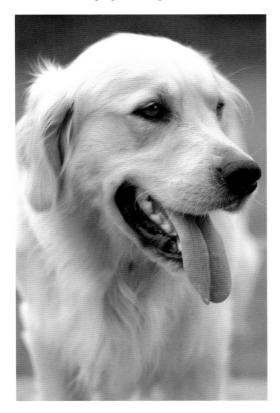

passed to humans. Sometimes an allergic reaction to the mite worsens the severe itching associated with sarcoptic mange.

■ Ear mites, *Otodectes cynotis*, lead to otodectic mange, which commonly affects the outer ear canal of the dog, though other areas can be affected as well. Your vet can prescribe a treatment to flush out the ears and kill any eggs in the ears. A complete month of treatment is necessary to cure this mange.

■ Two other mites, less common in dogs, include *Dermanyssus gallinae* (the "poultry" or "red" mite) and *Eutrombicula alfreddugesi* (the North American mite associated with trombiculidiasis or chigger infestation). The types of mange caused by both of these mites must be treated by vets.

INTERNAL PARASITES

Most animals — fish, birds and mammals, including dogs and humans — have worms and other parasites that live inside their bodies. According to Dr. Herbert R. Axelrod, a fish pathologist, there are two kinds of parasites: "smart" and "dumb." The smart parasites live in peaceful cooperation with their hosts — a symbiotic relationship — while the dumb parasites kill their hosts. Most worm infections are relatively easy to control. If they are not controlled, they weaken the host dog to the point that other medical problems occur, but they do not kill the host as dumb parasites would.

Roundworms: Roundworms that infect dogs live in the dog's intestines and shed eggs continually. It has been estimated that a dog produces about six or more ounces of feces every day and each ounce averages hundreds of thousands of roundworm eggs. There are no known areas in which dogs roam that do not contain roundworm eggs. Because roundworms infect people, too, it is wise to have your dog tested regularly.

A roundworm infection can kill puppies and cause severe problems in adult dogs, as the hatched larvae travel to the lungs and trachea through the bloodstream. Cleanliness is the best prevention against roundworms. Always pick up after your dog and dispose of feces in appropriate receptacles.

Hookworms: Hookworms are dangerous to humans as well as to dogs and cats, and can be the cause of severe iron-deficiency anemia. The worm uses its teeth to attach itself to the dog's intestines and changes the site of attachment about six times per day. Each time the worm repositions itself, the dog loses blood and can become anemic.

Symptoms of hookworm infection include dark stools, weight loss, general weakness, pale coloration and anemia, as well as possible skin problems. Fortunately, hookworms are easily purged with a number of medications that have proven effective. Discuss these with your veterinarian. Most heartworm preventives include a hookworm insecticide, as well.

Humans, can be infected by hookworms through exposure to contaminated feces. Because the worms cannot complete their life cycle on a human, the worms simply infest the skin and cause irritation. As a preventive, use disposable gloves or a poop scoop to pick up your dog's droppings and prevent your dog (or neighborhood cats) from defecating in children's play areas.

Tapeworms: There are many species of tapeworms, all of which are carried by fleas! Fleas are so small that your Golden could pass them onto your hands, your plate or your food, making it possible for you to ingest a flea that is carrying tapeworm eggs. While tapeworm infection is not life-threatening in dogs (it's a smart parasite!), it can be the cause of a serious liver disease in humans.

Whipworms: In North America, whipworms are among the most common parasitic worms in dogs. Affected dogs may experience upset tummies, colic and diarrhea. The worms, however, can live for months or years in the dog, beginning their larval stage in the small intestine, spending their adult life in the large intestine and finally passing infective eggs through the dog's feces. The only way to detect whipworms is with a fecal examination, though this is not always foolproof. Treatment for whipworms is tricky, due to the worms' unusual life cycle, and often dogs are reinfected due to exposure

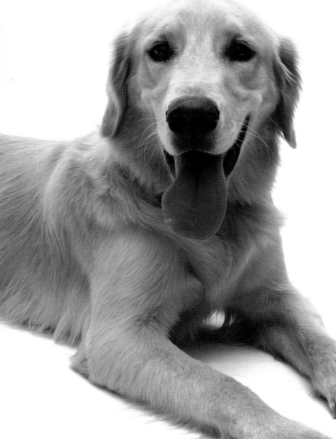

to infective eggs on the ground. Cleaning up droppings in your backyard and in public places is necessary for sanitary purposes and the health of your dog and others.

Threadworms: Though less common than roundworms, hookworms and the aforementioned parasites, threadworms concern dog owners in the southwestern United States and the Gulf Coast area where the climate is hot and humid.

Living in the small intestine of the dog, this worm measures a mere two milli-meters and is round in shape. Like the whipworm, the threadworm's life cycle is very complex and the eggs and larvae are transported through the feces.

A deadly disease in humans, threadworms readily infect people, mostly through the handling of feces. Threadworms are most often seen in young puppies. The most common symptoms include bloody diarrhea and pneumonia. Sick puppies must be isolated and treated immediately; vets recommend a follow-up treatment one month later.

Heartworms: Heartworms are thin, extended worms that measure up to 12 inches long and live in a dog's heart and the major blood vessels around it. Dogs may have up to 200 heartworms. Symptoms may be loss of energy, loss of appetite, coughing, the development of a pot belly and anemia.

Heartworms are transmitted by mosquitoes, which drink the blood of infected dogs and take in larvae with the blood. The larvae, called *microfilariae*, develop within the body of the mosquito and are then passed on to the next dog bitten after the larvae mature.

It takes two to three weeks for the larvae to develop to the infective stage within the body of the mosquito. Dogs are usually treated at about 6 weeks of age and maintained on a prophylactic dose given monthly.

Blood testing for heartworms is not necessarily indicative of how seriously your dog is infected. Although this is a dangerous disease, it is difficult for a dog to be infected. Discuss the various preventives with your vet, because there are many different types now available. Together you can decide on a safe course of prevention for your dog.

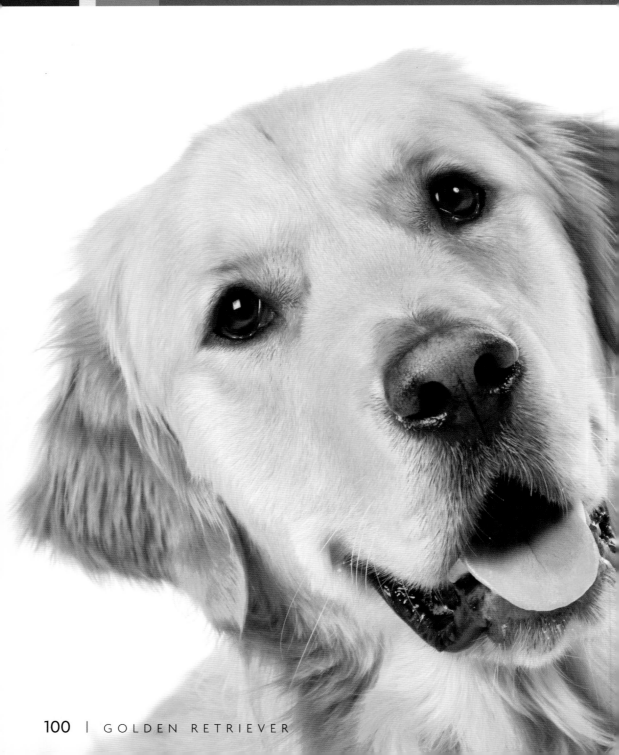

DINNER

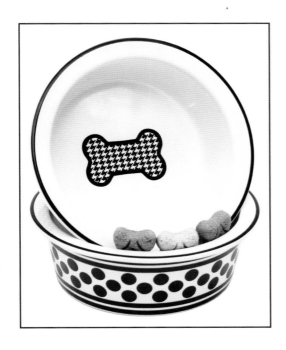

Y ou have probably heard it a thousand times: You are what you eat. Believe it or not, it is very true. For dogs, they are what you feed them because they have little choice in the matter. Even smart owners who want to feed their Goldens the best often cannot do so because it can be so confusing. With the overwhelming assortment of dog foods, it's difficult to figure out which one is truly best for their dogs.

BASIC TYPES

Dog foods are produced in various types: dry, wet, semimoist and frozen.

Dry food is useful for cost-conscious owners because it tends to be less expensive than others. These foods also contain the least fat and the most preservatives. Dry food is bulky and takes longer to eat than other foods, so it's more filling.

Wet food — available in cans or foil pouches — is usually 60 to 70 percent water and is more expensive than dry food. A palatable source of concentrated nutrition, wet food also makes a good supplement for underweight dogs or those recovering from illnesses. Some smart owners add a little wet food to dry food to increase its appeal.

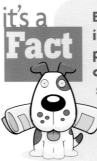

it's a **Fact** Bones can cause gastro-intestinal obstruction, perforation and may be contaminated with salmonella or E. coli. Leave them in the trash, and give your dog a nylon bone instead.

Semimoist food is flavorful, but it usually contains lots of sugar, which can lead to dental problems and obesity. Therefore, semimoist food is not a good choice for your Golden Retriever's main diet.

Frozen food is available in cooked and in raw forms and is usually more expensive than wet foods. The advantages of frozen food are similar to those of wet foods.

The amount of food that your Golden needs depends on a number of factors, such as his age, activity level, the quality of the food, reproductive status (if your Golden Retriever is a female) and size. What's the easiest way to figure it out? Start with the manufacturer's recommended amount, then adjust it according to your dog's response. For example, feed the recommended amount for a few weeks, and if your Golden loses weight, increase the amount by 10 to 20 percent. If your Golden gains weight, decrease the amount. It won't take long to determine the amount of food that keeps your best friend in optimal condition.

NUTRITION 101

All Goldens (and all dogs, for that matter) need proteins, carbohydrates, fats, vitamins and minerals to be in peak condition.

■ **Proteins** are used for growth and repair of muscles, bones and other tissues. They're also used for the production of antibodies, enzymes and hormones. All dogs need protein, but it's especially important for puppies because they grow and develop so quickly. Protein sources include various types of meat, meat meal, meat byproducts, eggs and dairy products.

■ **Carbohydrates** are metabolized into glucose, the body's principal energy source. Carbohydrates are available as sugars, starches and fiber.

• Sugars (simple carbohydrates) are not suitable nutrient sources for dogs.

• Starches — a preferred carbohydrate in dog food — are found in a variety of plant products. Starches must be cooked in order to be digested.

• Fiber (cellulose) — also a preferred type of carbohydrate found in dog food — isn't digestible, but helps the digestive tract function properly.

■ **Fats** are also a source of energy and play an important role in maintaining your Golden's skin and coat health, hormone production, nervous system function and vitamin transport. However, you must be aware of the fact that fats increase the palatability and the calorie count of dog food, which can lead to serious health problems, such as obesity, for

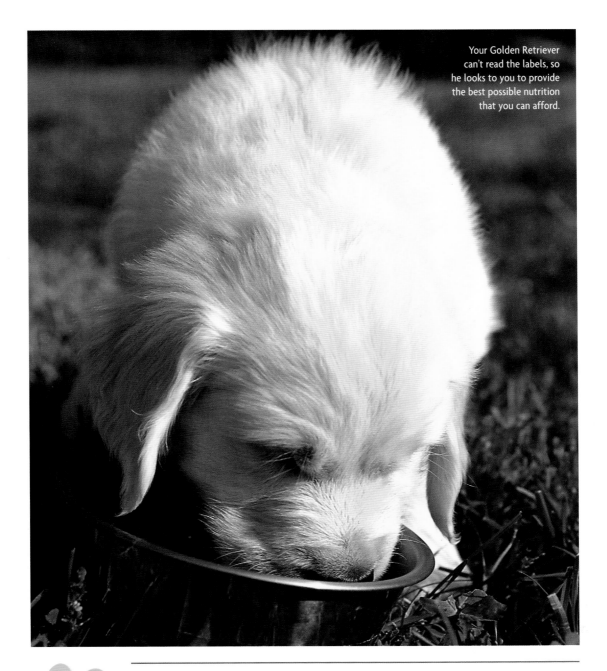

Your Golden Retriever can't read the labels, so he looks to you to provide the best possible nutrition that you can afford.

Believe it or not, during your Golden Retriever's lifetime, you'll buy a few thousand pounds of dog food. A growing Golden needs his chow! Go to **DogChannel.com/Club-Gold** and download a chart that outlines the average cost of dog food.

■ **Vitamins** and **minerals** are essential to dogs for proper muscle and nerve function, bone growth, healing, metabolism and fluid balance. Especially important for your Golden Retriever puppy are calcium, phosphorus and vitamin D, which must be supplied in the right balance to ensure proper development and maintenance of bones and teeth.

■ Just as your dog receives proper nutrition from his food, **water** is essential as well. Water keeps your dog's body hydrated and facilitates normal function of the body's systems. During housetraining, it is necessary to keep an eye on how much water your Golden Retriever is drinking, but once he is reliably trained, he should have access to clean, fresh water at all times, especially if you feed him dry food. Make sure that your dog's water bowl is clean, and change the water often.

puppies or dogs who are allowed to overindulge. Some foods contain added amounts of omega fatty acids such as docosohexaenoic acid, a compound that may enhance brain development and learning in puppies but is not considered an essential nutrient by the Association of American Feed Control Officials (www.aafco.org). Fats used in dog foods include tallow, lard, poultry fat, fish oil and vegetable oils.

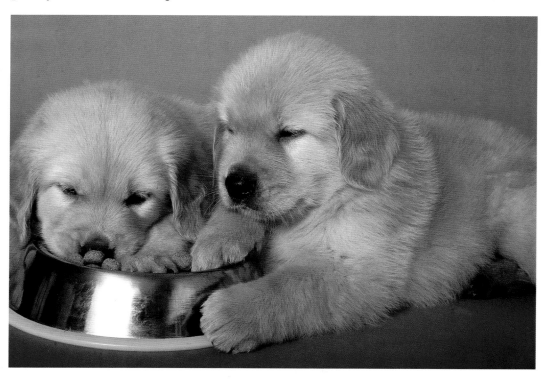

Dogs of all ages love treats and table food, but these goodies can unbalance your Golden Retriever's diet and lead to a weight problem if you don't feed him wisely. Table food, whether fed as a treat or as part of a meal, shouldn't account for more than 10 percent of your dog's daily caloric intake. If you plan to give your Golden treats, be sure to include "treat calories" when calculating the daily food requirement — so you don't end up with a pudgy pup!

When shopping for packaged treats, look for ones that provide complete nutrition. They're basically dog food in a fun form. Choose crunchy goodies for chewing fun and dental health. Other ideas for tasty treats include:

✓ small chunks of cooked, lean meat
✓ dry dog food morsels
✓ cheese
✓ veggies (cooked, raw or frozen)
✓ breads, crackers or dry cereal
✓ unsalted, unbuttered, plain, popped popcorn

Some foods, however, can be dangerous or even deadly to a dog. The following can cause digestive upset (vomiting or diarrhea) or fatal toxic reactions:

✗ **avocados:** if eaten in sufficient quantity these can cause gastrointestinal irritation, with vomiting and diarrhea

✗ **baby food:** may contain onion powder; does not provide balanced nutrition

✗ **chocolate:** contains methylxanthines and theobromine, caffeine-like compounds that can cause vomiting, diarrhea, heart abnormalities, tremors, seizures and death. Darker chocolates contain higher levels of the toxic compounds.

✗ **eggs, raw:** Whites contain an enzyme that prevents uptake of biotin, a B vitamin; may contain salmonella.

✗ **garlic (and related foods):** can cause gastrointestinal irritation and anemia if eaten in sufficient quantity

✗ **grapes:** can cause kidney failure if eaten in sufficient quantity (the toxic dose varies from dog to dog)

✗ **macadamia nuts:** can cause vomiting, weakness, lack of coordination and other problems

✗ **meat, raw:** may contain harmful bacteria such as salmonella or E. coli

✗ **milk:** can cause diarrhea in some puppies

✗ **onions (and related foods):** can cause gastrointestinal irritation and anemia if eaten in sufficient quantity

✗ **raisins:** can cause kidney failure if eaten in sufficient quantity (the toxic dose varies from dog to dog)

✗ **yeast bread dough:** can rise in the gastrointestinal tract, causing obstruction; produces alcohol as it rises

CHECK OUT THE LABEL

To help you get a feel for what you are feeding your dog, start by taking a look at the label on the package or can. Look for the words "complete and balanced." This tells you that the food meets specific nutritional requirements set by the AAFCO for either adults ("maintenance") or puppies and pregnant/lactating females ("growth and reproduction"). The label must state the group for which the food is intended. If you're feeding a puppy, choose a "growth and reproduction" food.

The nutrition label also includes a list of minimum protein, minimum fat, maximum fiber and maximum moisture content. (You won't find carbohydrate content because it's everything that isn't protein, fat, fiber and moisture.)

The nutritional analysis refers to crude protein and crude fat — amounts that have been determined in the laboratory. This analysis is technically accurate, but it does not tell you anything about digestibility: how much of the particular nutrient your Golden can actually use. For information about digestibility, contact the manufacturer (check the label for a telephone number and website address).

Virtually all commercial puppy foods exceed AAFCO's minimal requirements for protein and fat, the two nutrients most commonly evaluated when comparing foods. Protein levels in dry puppy foods usually range from about 26 to 30 percent; for canned foods, the values are about 9 to 13 percent. The fat content of dry puppy foods is about 20 percent or more; for canned foods, it's 8 percent or more. (Dry food values are larger than canned food values because dry food contains less water; the values are actually similar when compared on a dry matter basis.)

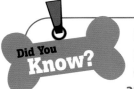

Did You Know? If you're feeding a puppy food that's complete and balanced, your young Golden Retriever doesn't need any dietary supplements such as vitamins, minerals or other types of food. In fact, dietary supplements could even harm your puppy by unbalancing his diet. If you have questions about supplementing your Golden's diet, ask your veterinarian.

Finally, check the ingredients on the label, which lists the ingredients in descending order by weight. Manufacturers are allowed to list separately different forms of a single ingredient (e.g., ground corn and corn gluten meal). The food may contain meat byproducts, meat and bone meal, and animal fat, which probably won't appeal to you but are nutritious and safe for your puppy. Higher quality foods usually have meat or meat products near the top of the ingredient list, but you don't need to worry about grain products as long as the label indicates that the food is nutritionally complete. Dogs are omnivores (not carnivores, as commonly believed), so all balanced dog foods contain animal and plant ingredients.

STORE IT RIGHT

Properly storing your Golden's food will ensure that it maintains its quality, nutrient content and taste. Here's what to do before and after you open that package or can.

◆ Dry food should be stored in a cool, dry, bug- and vermin-free place, especially if it's a preservative-free product. Many manufacturers include an expiration date on the package label, but this usually refers to the

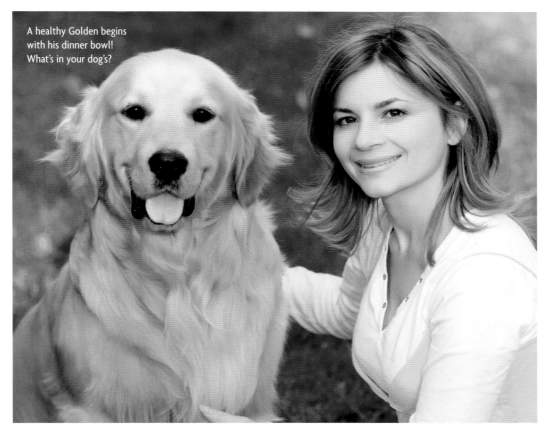

A healthy Golden begins with his dinner bowl! What's in your dog's?

shelf life of the unopened package. For optimal quality, don't buy more dry food than your Golden can eat in one month. To store dry food after opening the bag, fold the top down several times and secure it with a clip or, empty the contents into a food–grade airtight plastic container (check a pet-supply or discount store). Make sure the storage container is clean and dry and has never been used to store toxic materials.

◆ Canned food, if unopened, can remain good for three years or longer, but it's best to use it within one year of purchase. Discard puffy cans or those that are leaking fluid. Leftover canned food should be covered and refrigerated, then used within three days.

◆ Frozen food can be stored for at least one year in the freezer. Longer storage can cause deterioration of the quality and taste of the food. Thaw frozen food in the refrigerator or use the defrost setting of your microwave. Cover and refrigerate leftovers, which should be used within 24 hours.

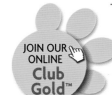

GASTRIC DILATATION-VOLVULUS

Gastric dilatation-volvulus (also known as "bloat") is a feeding-related disorder that most commonly affects large, deep-chested dogs. As the name indicates, the disorder has two components: gastric dilatation — an excessive accumulation of gas and fluid in the stomach — and volvulus — a twisting of the stomach, which can occur if the dilatation is not relieved.

The most prominent sign of GDV is a severely distended abdomen that sounds like a drum when tapped. Afflicted dogs are restless and uncomfortable and may vomit without bringing anything up. The disorder worsens rapidly; prompt veterinary attention is required to prevent circulatory collapse (shock) and death. Home remedies for GDV are not effective.

Several factors increase a dog's risk of developing GDV, including deep-chested conformation, having a first-degree relative (parent, sibling or offspring) affected by GDV, age (older dogs are more susceptible), nervous personality, rapid eating, large meals, high-fat foods (those listing fat as one of the first several ingredients), meals composed solely of dry food and eating from a raised dish. Despite the belief that water consumption during or after eating and exercise after eating can cause GDV, the role of these factors, if any, has not been clearly proven.

To reduce the risk of GDV, feed your Golden a combination of dry and canned food (not high-fat) from a dish placed on the floor. Encourage slower eating by feeding at least twice a day. If necessary, put an 8- to 10-inch piece of sturdy chain (1-inch links) in the food bowl — your Golden will have to slow down to pick the food from around the chain. Avoid stressful situations before and after mealtime.

STAGES OF LIFE

When selecting your dog's diet, three stages of development must be considered: the puppy stage, the adult stage and the senior stage.

Puppy Diets: Pups instinctively want to nurse, and a normal puppy will exhibit this behavior from just a few moments following birth. Puppies should be allowed to nurse for about the first six weeks, although by the third or fourth week, the breeder will begin to introduce small portions of suitable solid food. Most breeders like to initially introduce alternate milk and solid-food meals, leading up to weaning time.

By the time Golden Retriever puppies are 7 weeks old (or a maximum of 8), they should be fully weaned and fed solely on puppy food. Selection of the most suitable, high-quality food at this time is essential because a puppy's fastest growth rate is during the first year of life. Seek advice about your dog's diet from your veterinarian. The frequency of meals will be reduced over time, and when a young dog has reached 10 to 12 months, he should be switched to an adult diet.

Puppy and junior diets can be well balanced for the needs of your Golden so that, except in certain circumstances, additional

SMART TIP!

How can you tell if your Golden Retriever is fit or fat? When you run your hands down your pal's sides from front to back, you should be able to easily feel her ribs. It's fine if you feel a little body fat (and a lot of hair), but you shouldn't feel huge fat pads. You should also be able to feel your Golden's waist — an indentation behind the ribs.

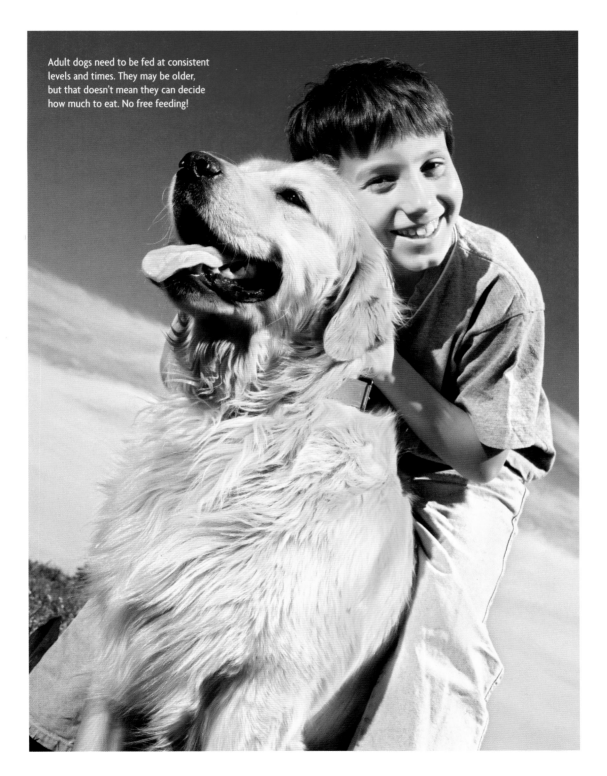

Adult dogs need to be fed at consistent levels and times. They may be older, but that doesn't mean they can decide how much to eat. No free feeding!

vitamin, mineral and protein supplements will not be required.

How often should you feed your Golden in a day? Puppies have small stomachs and high metabolic rates, so they need to eat several times a day to consume sufficient nutrients. If your puppy is younger than 3 months old, feed him four or five meals a day. When your Golden is 3 to 5 months old, decrease the number of meals to three or four. At 6 months, most puppies can move to an adult schedule of two meals a day.

Adult Diets: A dog is considered an adult when he has stopped growing. Rely on your veterinarian or canine dietary specialist to recommend an acceptable maintenance diet. Major dog food manufacturers specialize in this type of food, and smart owners must select the one best suited to their dogs' needs. Do not leave food out all day for "free-choice" feeding, as this freedom inevitably translates to inches around your dog's waist.

Senior Diets: As dogs get older, their metabolism begins to change. A senior Golden Retriever usually exercises less, moves more slowly and sleeps more. This change in his lifestyle and physiological performance requires a change in diet. Because these changes take place slowly, they might not be recognizable at first. These metabolic changes increase the tendency toward obesity, requiring an even more vigilant approach to feeding. Obesity in an older dog exacerbates the health problems that already accompany old age.

As a Golden ages, few of his organs function up to par. The kidneys slow down, and the intestines become less efficient. These age-related factors are best handled with a change in diet and a change in feeding schedule to give smaller portions that are more easily digested.

There is no single best diet for an older Golden Retriever. While many older dogs will do perfectly fine on light or senior diets, other dogs will do better on special premium diets such as lamb and rice. Be sensitive to your senior Golden's diet, and this will help control other problems that may arise with your old friend.

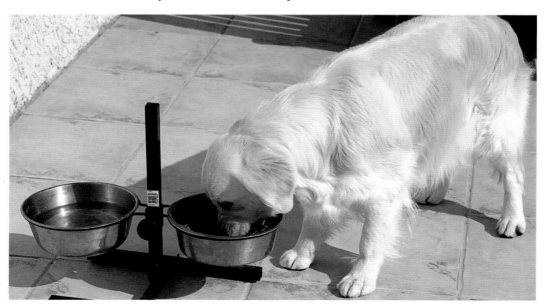

These delicious, dog-friendly recipes will have your furry friend smacking her lips and salivating for more. Just remember: Treats aren't meant to replace your dog's regular meals. Give your Golden Retriever snacks sparingly and continue to feed her nutritious, well-balanced meals.

Cheddar Squares

$\frac{1}{3}$ cup all-natural applesauce
$\frac{1}{3}$ cup low-fat cheddar cheese, shredded
$\frac{1}{3}$ cup water
2 cups unbleached white flour

In a medium bowl, mix all the wet ingredients. In a large bowl, mix the flour. Slowly add all the wet ingredients to the flour. Mix well. Pour batter into a greased, 13x9x2-inch pan. Bake at 375-degrees Fahrenheit for 25 to 30 minutes. Bars are done when a toothpick inserted in the center and removed comes out clean. Cool and cut into bars. This recipe makes about 54, 1$\frac{1}{2}$-inch bars.

Peanut Butter Bites

3 tablespoons vegetable oil
$\frac{1}{4}$ cup smooth peanut butter, no salt or sugar
$\frac{1}{4}$ cup honey
1$\frac{1}{2}$ teaspoon baking powder
2 eggs
2 cups whole wheat flour

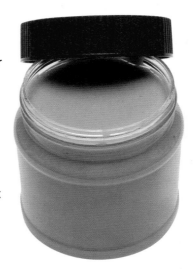

In a large bowl, mix all ingredients until dough is firm. If the dough is too sticky, mix in a small amount of flour. Knead dough on a lightly floured surface until firm. Roll out dough half an inch thick, and cut with cookie cutters. Put cookies on a cookie sheet half an inch apart. Bake at 350-degrees Fahrenheit for 20 to 25 minutes. When done, cookies should be firm to the touch. Turn oven off and leave cookies for one to two hours to harden. This recipe makes about 40, 2-inch-long cookies.

CHAPTER 9

GROOMING

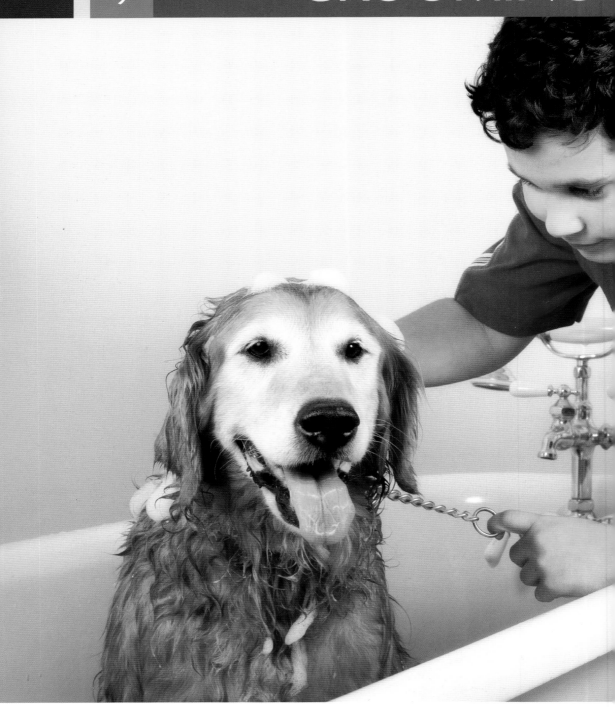

GOLDILOCKS

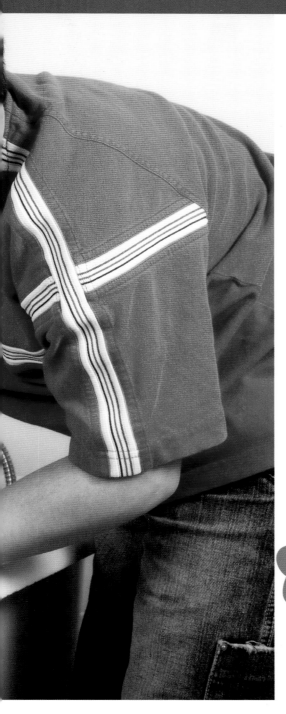

Like living rays of sunshine, Golden Retrievers bring warmth, joy and beauty into the lives of their owners. Despite some claims that Goldens have a self-cleaning coat, a Golden's luxuriant fur requires frequent brushing, combing and shampooing. When you are socializing your pup or when your adult dog is shedding, for example, daily brushing is best. In addition, due to their energetic outdoor forays, Goldens also need frequent de-burring, de-ticking and de-twigging. As inveterate nature lovers, they consider skunks irresistible and relish a roll in the smelliest stuff they can dig up.

GET STARTED

The first step in a grooming routine is brushing. Golden Retrievers are notorious shedders, and regular brushing cuts down on the amount of hair left on floors and furniture. It also prevents painful mats from forming in their coats. (If your friends are repelled by a little — OK maybe more than a little — dog hair, you may have to find a new set of friends.) These dogs tend to shed moderately year-round and blow coat (shed their

Did You Know? Nail clipping can be tricky, so many dog owners leave the task to professionals. However, if you walk your Golden on concrete, you may not have to worry. The concrete will act like a nail file and will help keep the nails neatly trimmed.

entire coat profusely) during each spring and fall season.

Scheduling brush time after daily walks allowing you to check for mats, leaves and burrs. Start with your dog's hindquarters, brushing around his body. You may use a pin brush on the feathering, but groomers prefer a slicker brush with curved metal bristles.

Be careful not to scratch sensitive skin. With his desire to please and high threshold for pain, a Golden may not react to harsh brushing, but his skin can be easily slicker-burned by heavy-handed brushing.

The next step is to check your work with a double-sided stainless steel comb, removing any hair that your brush may have missed. This is also a good time to check the coat for fleas, ticks and skin problems. A fine-toothed flea comb aids in this process. Look particularly for hot spots: open, oozing sores some-times caused by allergies to fleas, food or hormonal changes. Hot spots appear most often in warm, humid weather, and Goldens are prone to them. These spots heal best if the area is shaved and treated with an antibiotic topical solution that promotes drying.

Regularly groom your puppy, even though he may not be shedding, to help cement the bond between you. Use a gentle slicker brush with straight wire bristles, and groom daily until your puppy grows accustomed to it. Keep the sessions short, and don't expect perfect behavior from your wiggly, playful pup.

The goal of this early canine grooming is to teach your dog to stand quietly while you handle every part of its body. Mastering the come and sit cues will also make grooming much easier throughout your Golden Retriever's life. When your Golden puppy is

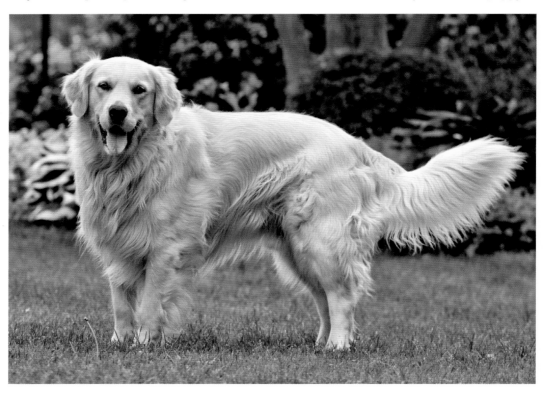

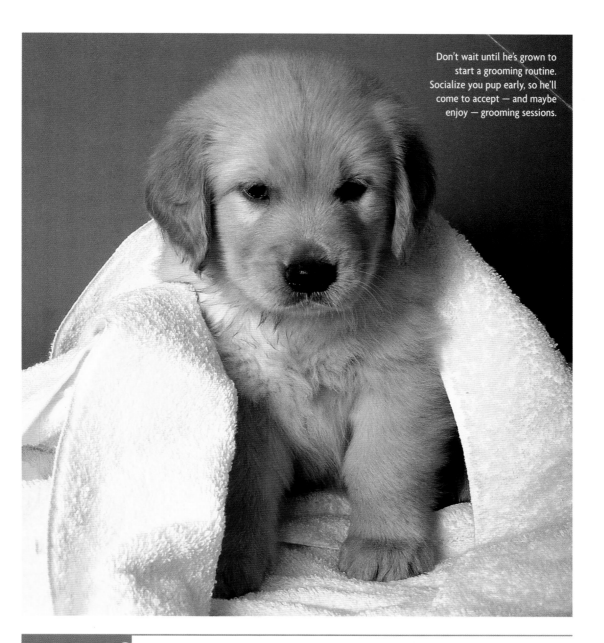

Don't wait until he's grown to start a grooming routine. Socialize you pup early, so he'll come to accept — and maybe enjoy — grooming sessions.

After removing a tick, clean your dog's skin with hydrogen peroxide. If Lyme disease is common where you live, have your veterinarian test the tick. Tick preventive medication will discourage ticks from attaching and kill any that do.

— groomer Andrea Vilardi from West Paterson, N.J.

small, it may be easier to hold him in your lap, but also ask him to stand up for part of the session, either on the floor or on a grooming table.

NAILING THINGS DOWN

The best time to clip your dog's nails is immediately after a bath because the water will have softened the nails, and your Golden may be somewhat tired-out by the bath. Nail trimming is recommended every two weeks, using nail clippers or a nail grinding tool.

Trimming nails are crucial to maintaining the Golden Retriever's normal foot shape. Long nails can permanently damage a dog's feet; the tight ligaments of round, arched feet will break down more quickly. If your dog's nails are clicking on the floor, they need trimming.

Your Golden should be accustomed to having his nails trimmed at an early age because it will be part of your maintenance routine throughout his life. Not only do neatly trimmed nails look nicer, but long nails can unintentionally scratch someone. Also, long nails have a better chance of ripping and bleeding, or causing your Golden's toes to spread.

Before you start clipping, make sure you can identify the quick in each nail (the vein in the center of each nail). It will bleed if accidentally cut, which will be painful for your dog since it contains a web of nerve endings. Keep some type of clotting agent on hand, such as a styptic pencil or styptic powder (the type used for shaving). This will quickly stop the bleeding when applied to the end of the cut nail. Do not panic if this happens, just stop the bleeding and talk soothingly to your dog. Once he has calmed down, move on to the next nail. It is better to clip a little at a time, particularly with dogs who have dark nails, where the quick isn't easily visible.

Hold your dog steady as you begin trimming his nails; you do not want him to make any sudden movements or run away. Talk to him calmly and stroke him as you clip. Holding his foot in your hand, simply take off the end of each nail in one quick clip. You can purchase nail clippers that are specifically made for dogs at pet-supply stores.

There are two predominant types of clippers. One is the guillotine clipper, which is a hole with a blade in the middle. Using this tool, squeeze the handles so that the blade meets the nail and chops it off. It sounds gruesome, and for some dogs, it is utterly intolerable. Scissor-type clippers are gentler on the nail. The important thing to make sure of is that the blades on either of these clippers are sharp. Once you are at the desired length, use a nail file to smooth the rough edges of the nails so they don't catch on carpeting or outdoor debris.

A third option is a cordless nail grinder fitted with a fine grade (100 grit) sandpaper cylinder. Stone cylinders are more prone to heat buildup and vibration. When grinding, use a low-speed (5,000 to 10,000 rpm). Hold your dog's paw firmly in one hand spreading the toes slightly apart. Touch the spinning grinder wheel to the nail tip for one or two seconds without applying pressure. Repeat if necessary to remove the nail tip protruding

it's a Fact

Shedding naturally occurs in the spring and fall, and for females, after each estrus (heat) cycle. It also can occur in times of illness, stress and excitement.

beyond the quick. Grinders have the added benefit of leaving nails smooth and free of sharp, jagged edges that traditional nail clippers leave behind.

If the procedure becomes more than you can deal with, just remember: Groomers and veterinarians charge a nominal fee to clip nails. By using their services, you won't have to see your pet glower at you for the rest of the night.

When inspecting paws, you must check not only your dog's nails but also the pads. Check to see that the pads have not become cracked and always inspect between the pads to be sure nothing has become lodged there. Depending upon the season, there may be a danger of grass seeds or thorns becoming embedded, or even tar from the road. Butter, by the way, is useful in removing tar from your Golden Retriever's feet.

THE EARS HAVE IT

As you perform your grooming routine, your puppy should become acclimated to you looking in his ears and examining his mouth. The combination of the Golden's

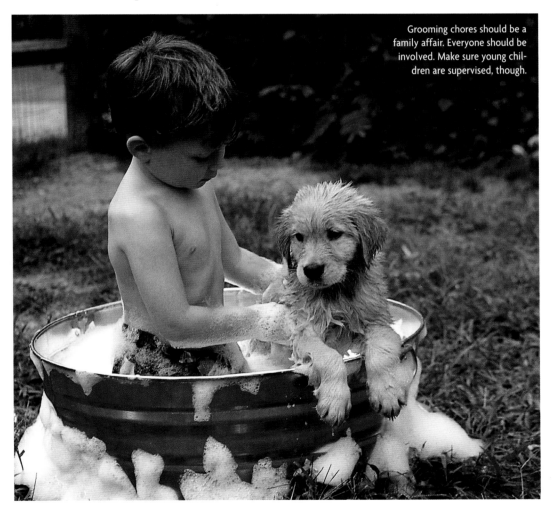

Grooming chores should be a family affair. Everyone should be involved. Make sure young children are supervised, though.

drop ears, which provide a warm, dark haven in which bacteria flourish, and their love of swimming makes ear infections fairly common in this breed. Look way down inside your dog's ears. Do you see just a little tan wax? That's fine; leave it. Do you see gobs of gunk? That's not OK.

If your Golden is constantly scratching his ears and shaking his head, take a close look at that gunk. Place some on a piece of black paper and look at it with a magnifying glass. If you see little white moving specks, your dog has ear mites. You'll need a veterinarian to confirm your diagnosis, so that he or she can prescribe a proper and effective treatment that won't damage your dog's ears.

If your Golden Retriever tilts his head and acts like his ear hurts, or if the ear appears red and swollen, it's time to see the veterinarian. You don't want to clean his ears if he's in pain or if there's a chance of a perforated eardrum.

Assuming your Golden Retriever just has dirty ears, cleaning them is quite simple; cleaning solution is readily available at pet-supply stores. Quickly squeeze some of the cleaning solution into your dog's ear; if you go slowly, the solution will tickle and he'll shake it right out. Keep your hand on the base of the ear, and massage the liquid in so it squishes all around. Your Golden will shake the liquid out, flinging dissolved gunk all over the place, so you may want to do this outdoors. Wipe clean any goop hanging on the ears with a cotton ball. For really dirty ears, do this several times in the course of a week.

Don't stick cotton swabs into your Golden Retriever's ears. They can irritate the skin, pack gunk more tightly or perforate the eardrum. Don't use powders, which will mix with moisture and form a hard cake. Don't use hydrogen peroxide, which will leave the ear moist; and most of all, don't be overzealous in your cleaning. More problems are caused by owners stripping the ears of natural waxes than by neglecting to clean them.

A gentle cleaning once a week helps to prevent ear problems. Routine cleaning is a preventive measure; it will not clear up an existing infection and may even make it worse. If you notice that the hair under, behind or on top of your Golden's ears is too profuse, de-bulk the fur with thinning shears to better frame that beautiful Golden face.

BEFORE GETTING WET

Before administering the final spit and polish of a bath, be sure your Golden's coat is thoroughly brushed out. Once you add water, mats in the coat tend to tighten and multiply. If matting is a problem, purchase a mat comb or mat breaker, a small tool with removable teeth. These slice right through the mats, allowing you to easily remove them with your comb or brush. Use these sharp instruments carefully, though, making short strokes in the direction in which the hair grows. Twisting them near ear leathers or using them on skin flaps or bone can injure your dog.

Never cut mats with scissors — a sudden move from your dog could be disastrous. The most common places for mats to form

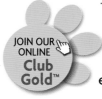

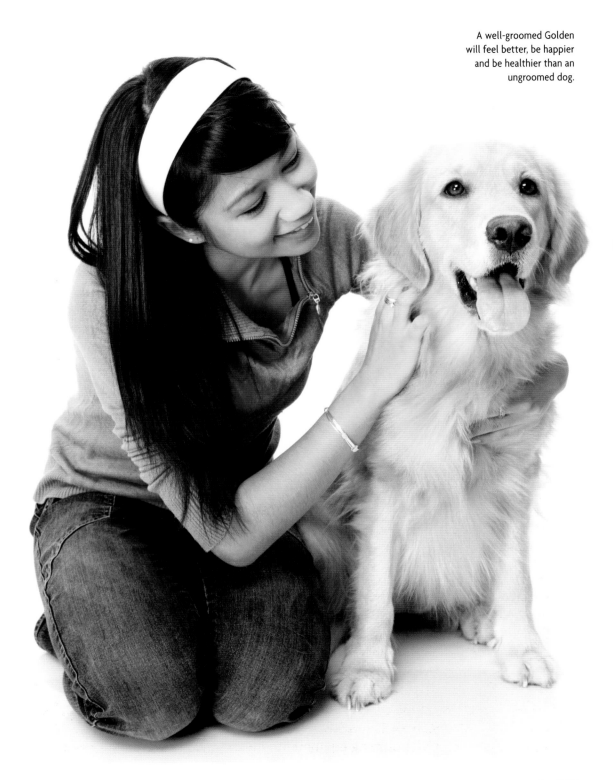

A well-groomed Golden will feel better, be happier and be healthier than an ungroomed dog.

are behind the ears, along rear feathering, on the undersides or "skirts" and in the tail. Keep your pet free of mats to avoid skin irritation and places for fleas to set up housekeeping.

While feet may be trimmed and stray hairs neatened, the Golden Retriever is shown in the ring in its natural state, unaltered by cutting or clipping. For pets, on the other hand, the grooming shop may thin and trim the Golden coat to make it easier for the owner to maintain between groomings. Although purists may balk, clients love the look because it preserves the Golden's beauty without resorting to clipping the coat down. Shaving your Golden is not recommended, although a few owners whose dogs spend their summers in the pool or the lake insist upon it.

If your grooming has uncovered fleas or flea debris — those tell-tale black specks that

look like pepper — you'll need a flea shampoo. Several good products on the market use botanical ingredients, such as pyrethrins, neem, citronella, d-limonene and tea tree oil (also called melaluca). Other combination products contain a chemical synergist such as permethrin, a man-made pyrethrin. Reserve the use of strong chemical dips only for extreme cases of infestation.

All such shampoos need to be left on the coat for a full 15 minutes before rinsing thoroughly. Unfortunately, fleas on the pet usually indicate fleas in the home, so you

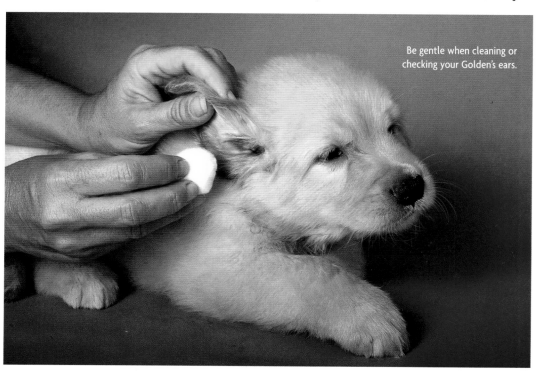

Be gentle when cleaning or checking your Golden's ears.

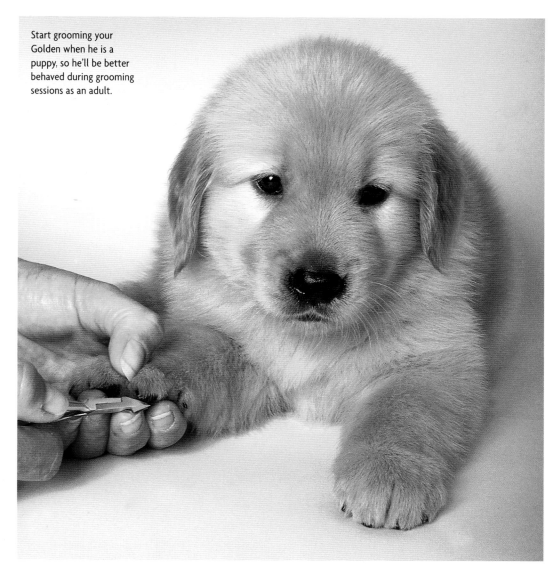

Start grooming your Golden when he is a puppy, so he'll be better behaved during grooming sessions as an adult.

will need foggers, sprays, powders or the services of a professional exterminator to complete your flea-eradication efforts.

LATHER UP

Always use a shampoo made specifically for dogs. Human hair-care products or household detergents dry out the skin and coat. Sometimes a sponge bath suffices, just hosing down the legs, undersides and rear feathers. Other times a good brushing is all it takes to remove dried dirt and debris.

On puppies, a mild tearless shampoo works best, while a high-quality basic shampoo is fine for adults. If unpleasant doggie odors from outdoor adventures are a problem, you may use a deodorizing or fragrance-enhanced shampoo. A medicated product such as oatmeal shampoo helps relieve dandruff and dry skin.

Your Golden Retriever shouldn't be caught in the middle of a power struggle between the children and the parents. Divvy up grooming and bathing responsibilities early on, and make the issue non-negotiable. A clean Golden will be welcomed into the house; a dirty one is banished to the backyard, always on the outside looking in. Even breeds that are low-maintenance, such as Goldens, need some regular grooming.

Young pups can be bathed right in the sink, while adults may be bathed in the bathtub using a hand-held shower attachment. Once your pet is thoroughly rinsed, use a towel to get him as dry as possible, then complete the process with your hand-held dryer on a low setting.

Be careful not to hold the air flow too long or too close on any given area because dryers get very hot and could easily burn your dog's skin. A final brushing after your dog has been dried removes more dead coat and fluffs up that beautiful golden fur. Never let your damp Golden outdoors — the first thing he will do is find a nice pile of dirt to roll in.

The same effort that is put into grooming during puppyhood should carry over into your Golden's senior years, from age 9 onward when these faithful friends exhibit an endearing white "clown" face. They require just as much grooming care in their old age, but be very gentle: Those old bones and joints tend to stiffen with arthritis. Their coats also dry out and benefit from medicated shampoos.

If you give your Golden the care he needs, you will be rewarded with a friendship that will enrich your life beyond words. A large part of that care is proper grooming. If you're not up to it yourself, have your Golden professionally groomed every six to 12 weeks with routine home grooming in between visits. Goldens soak up attention like a sponge and will revel in the attention of frequent grooming sessions.

IT'S THE TOOTH

Like people, Golden Retrievers can suffer from dental disease, so experts recommend regular teeth cleanings. Daily brushing is best, but your dog will benefit from having his teeth brushed a few times a week. The teeth should be white and free of yellowish tartar and the gums should appear healthy and pink. Gums that bleed easily when you perform dental duties may have gingivitis.

The first thing to know is that your puppy probably isn't going to want your fingers in his mouth. Desensitizing your puppy — getting

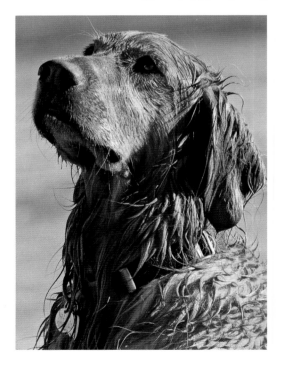

him to accept that you will be looking at and touching his teeth — is the first step to overcoming his resistance. You can begin this as soon as you get your puppy, with the help of the thing that motivates dogs the most: food.

For starters, let your puppy lick some chicken, vegetable or beef broth off your finger. Then, dip your finger in broth again, and gently insert your finger in the side of your dog's mouth. Touch his side teeth and gums. Several sessions will get your puppy used to having his mouth touched.

SMART TIP!

Don't forget to trim the dewclaws, those thumb-like nails on the inside of the front legs. You may also wish to snip the hair between your dog's pads with small, straight scissors and trim her tops of the feet with thinning shears to avoid those hairy tufts sometimes referred to as "Golden bedroom slippers."

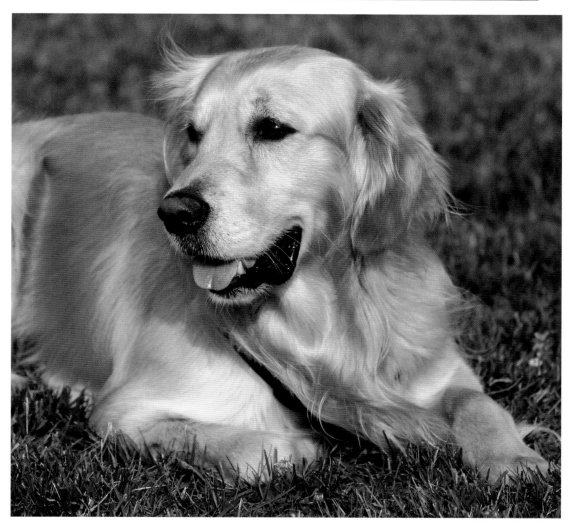

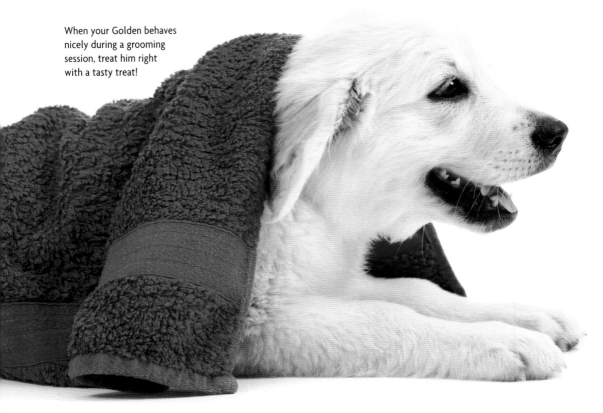

When your Golden behaves nicely during a grooming session, treat him right with a tasty treat!

Use a toothbrush specifically made for a dog or a fingertip brush to brush your Golden Retriever's teeth. Hold his mouth with the one hand, and brush with the other. Use toothpaste formulated for dogs with delectable flavors like poultry and beef. Human toothpaste froths too much and can give your dog an upset stomach. Brush in a circular motion with the brush held at a 45-degree angle to the gum line. Be sure to get the fronts, tops and sides of each tooth.

Check the teeth for signs of plaque, tartar or gum disease, including redness, swelling, foul breath, discolored enamel near the gum line and receding gums. If you see these, immediately take your Golden Retriever to the veterinarian.

REWARD A JOB WELL DONE

Rewarding your Golden Retriever for behaving during grooming is the best way to ensure stress-free grooming throughout his lifetime. Bathing energizes your pet, and using the time immediately after grooming as play time is the best way to reward your Golden for a job well done. Watching your clean, healthy Golden tear from room to room in sheer joy is your reward for being a caring owner.

it's a **Fact**

Dogs can't rinse and spit after a brushing, so doggie toothpaste must be safe for pets to swallow. Always use a toothpaste specially formulated for dogs when brushing your Golden's teeth.

Six Tips for Golden Care

1. Grooming tools can be scary to some dogs, so let yours see and sniff everything at the start. Keep your beauty sessions short, too. Most retrievers don't enjoy standing still for too long.

2. Look at your dog's eyes for any discharge and her ears for inflammation, debris or foul odor. If you notice anything that doesn't look right, immediately contact your veterinarian.

3. Choose a time to groom your dog when you don't have to rush, and assemble all of the grooming tools before you begin. This way you can focus on your dog's needs instead of having to stop in the middle of the session to search for an item.

4. Start establishing a grooming routine the day after you bring her home. A regular grooming schedule will make it easier to remember what touch-up your dog needs.

5. Proper nail care helps with your dog's gait and spinal alignment. Nails that are too long can force a dog to walk improperly. Also, too-long nails can snag and tear, causing painful injury to your Golden Retriever.

6. Good dental health prevents gum disease and early tooth loss. Brush your Golden's teeth daily and see a veterinarian yearly.

Six Questions to Ask a Groomer

1. Do you cage dry? Are you willing to hand dry or air dry my pet?

2. What type of shampoo are you using? Is it tearless? If not, do you have a tearless variety available for use?

3. Will you restrain my pet if she acts up during nail clipping? What methods do you use to handle difficult dogs?

4. Are you familiar with the Golden Retriever breed? Do you have any references from other Golden owners?

5. Is the shop air-conditioned during hot weather?

6. Will my dog be getting brushed or just bathed?

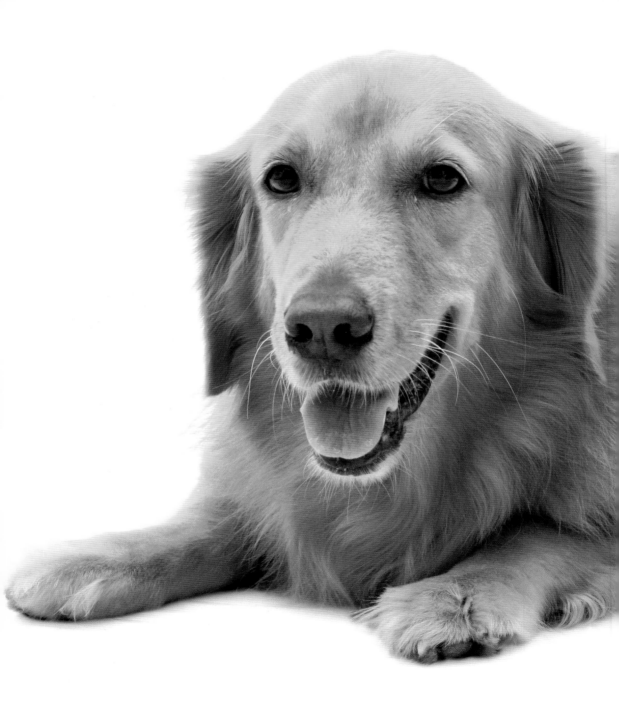

TRAIN

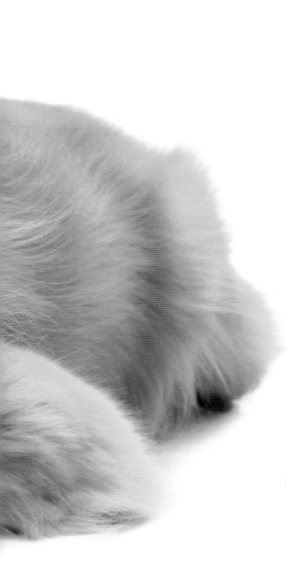

Reward-based training methods — clicking and luring — instruct dogs on what to do and help them do it correctly, setting them up for success and rewards rather than mistakes and punishment.

CLICK THIS!

A clicker is a small, plastic device that makes a sharp clicking sound when a button is pressed. You can purchase them at any pet-supply store. It is used in a training method that precisely marks a desired behavior so your dog knows exactly which behavior earned a reward.

When using a clicker, you "charge" the clicker by clicking and giving your Golden Retriever a treat several times, until he understands that the click means he gets a treat. The click then becomes a secondary reinforcer. It's not the reward itself, but it will become so closely linked with a reward in your dog's mind that it has the same effect as a reward.

Next, click the clicker when your Golden performs any desirable behavior. Then, you follow it up with a click and treat. The click

Did You Know? The prime period for socialization is short. Most behavior experts agree that positive experiences period between 4 and 14 weeks of age are vital to the development of a puppy who'll grow into an adult dog with a sound temperament.

marks, more exact than a word or gesture, the desired behavior, quickly teaching your dog which behaviors will earn rewards.

Most dogs find food rewards meaningful; Goldens are no exception as they tend to be food motivated. This works well because positive training relies on using treats, at least initially, to encourage a dog to demonstrate a certain behavior. The treat is then given as a reward. When you reinforce desired behaviors with rewards that are valuable to your dog, you are met with happy cooperation rather than resistance.

Positive reinforcement does not necessarily equal passivity. While you are rewarding your Golden Retriever's desirable behaviors, you must still manage him to be sure he isn't getting rewarded for his undesirable behaviors. Training tools, such as leashes, tethers, baby gates and crates, help keep your dog out of trouble. The use of force-free negative punishment (the dog's behavior makes a good thing go away) helps him realize there are negative consequences for inappropriate behaviors.

LEARNING SOCIAL GRACES

Now that you have done all of the preparatory work and have helped your Golden get accustomed to his new home and family, it's time for you to have some fun! Socializing your pup gives you the opportunity to show off your new friend, and your Golden gets to reap the benefits of being an adorable little creature whom people will want to pet and gush over how precious he is.

Besides getting to know his new family, your puppy should be exposed to other people, animals and situations; but, of course, he must not come into close contact with dogs whom you don't know until he has had all his vaccinations. This will help him become well adjusted as he grows up and less prone to being timid or fearful of the new things he will encounter.

Your puppy's socialization began at the breeder's home, but now it is your responsibility to continue it. The socialization he receives until he is 12 weeks of age is the most critical, as this is the time when he forms his impressions of the outside world. Be very careful during the 8- to 10-week period, also known as the "fear period." The interaction he receives during this time should be gentle and reassuring. Puppies require a lot of human contact, affection, handling and exposure to other animals. Lack of socialization can manifest itself in fear and aggression as your Golden matures.

Once your Golden Retriever has received his necessary vaccinations, feel free to take him out and about (on his leash, of course). Walk him around the neighborhood, take him on your daily errands, let people pet him and let him meet other dogs and pets. Make sure to expose your Golden to different people — men, women, kids, babies, men with beards, teenagers with cell phones or riding skateboards, joggers, shoppers, someone in a wheelchair, a pregnant woman, etc. Make sure your Golden explores different surfaces like sidewalks, gravel and even a puddle. Positive experience is the key to building confidence. It's up to you to make sure your Golden safely discovers the world so he will be a calm, confident and well-socialized dog.

It's important that you take the lead in all socialization experiences and never put your pup in a scary or potentially harmful situation. Be mindful of your Golden's limitations. Fifteen minutes at a public market is fine; two hours at a loud outdoor concert is too much. Meeting vaccinated, tolerant and gentle older dogs is great. Meeting dogs whom you don't know or trust isn't a great idea, especially if they appear very energetic, dominant or fearful. Control the situations in which you place your puppy.

The best way to socialize your puppy to a new experience is to make him think it's the best thing ever. You can do this with a lot of happy talk, enthusiasm and, of course, food. To convince your puppy that almost any experience is a blast, always carry treats. Consider carrying two types — a bag of his puppy chow, which you can give him when introducing him to nonthreatening experiences, and a bag of high-value, mouthwatering treats to give him when introducing him to unfamiliar experiences.

SMART TIP!

If your Golden Retriever refuses to sit with both haunches squarely beneath her and instead sits on one side or the other, she may have a physical reason for doing so. Discuss the habit with your veterinarian to be certain your dog isn't suffering from some structural problem.

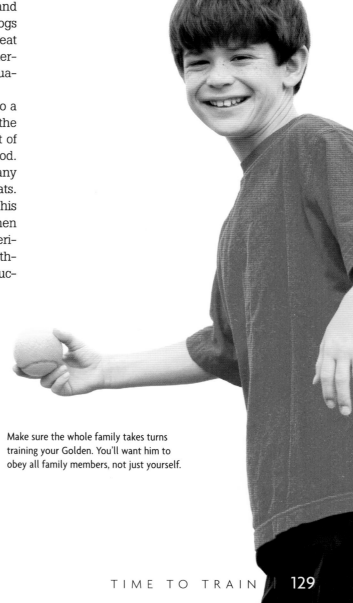

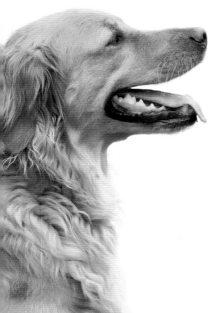

Make sure the whole family takes turns training your Golden. You'll want him to obey all family members, not just yourself.

BASIC CUES

All Goldens, regardless of your training and relationship goals, need to know at least five basic good-manner behaviors: sit, down, stay, come and heel. Here are tips for teaching your Golden these important cues.

SIT: Every dog should learn to sit.

• Hold a treat at the end of your Golden Retriever's nose.

• Move the treat over his head.

• When your dog sits, click a clicker or say "Yes!"

• Feed your dog the treat.

• If your dog jumps up, hold the treat lower. If he backs up, back him into a corner and wait until he sits. Be patient. Keep your clicker handy and click (or say "Yes!") and treat anytime he offers a sit.

• When he is able to easily offers sits, say "sit" just before he does, so he can make the association between the word and the behavior. Add the sit cue when you know you can get the behavior. Your dog doesn't know what the word means until you repeatedly associate it with the appropriate behavior.

• When your Golden easily sits on cue, start using intermittent reinforcement by clicking some sits but not others. At first, click most sits and skip an occasional one (this is a high rate of reinforcement). Gradually make your clicks random.

DOWN: If your Golden can sit, then he can learn to lie down.

◆ Have your Golden sit.

◆ Hold the treat in front of his nose. Move it down slowly, straight toward the floor (toward his toes). If he follows all the way down, click and treat.

◆ If he gets stuck, move the treat down slowly. Click and treat for small movements downward — moving his head a bit lower, or inching one paw forward. Keep clicking and treating until your Golden is all the way down. This training method is called "shaping" — rewarding small pieces of a behavior until your dog succeeds.

◆ If your dog stands as you move the treat toward the floor, have him sit, and move the treat even more slowly downward, shaping with clicks and treats for small, downward movements. If he stands, cheerfully say "Oops!" (which means "Sorry, no treat for that!"), have him sit and try again.

◆ If shaping isn't working, sit on the floor with your knee raised. Have your Golden sit next to you. Put your hand with the treat under your knee and lure him under your leg so he lies down and crawls to follow the treat. Click and treat!

◆ When you can lure the down easily, add the verbal cue, wait a few seconds to let your dog think, then lure him down to show him the association. Repeat until your Golden goes down on the verbal cue; then begin using intermittent reinforcement.

STAY: What good are sit and down cues if your dog doesn't stay?

▲ Start with your Golden Retriever in a sit or down position.

▲ Put the treat in front of your dog's nose and keep it there.

▲ Click and reward several times while he

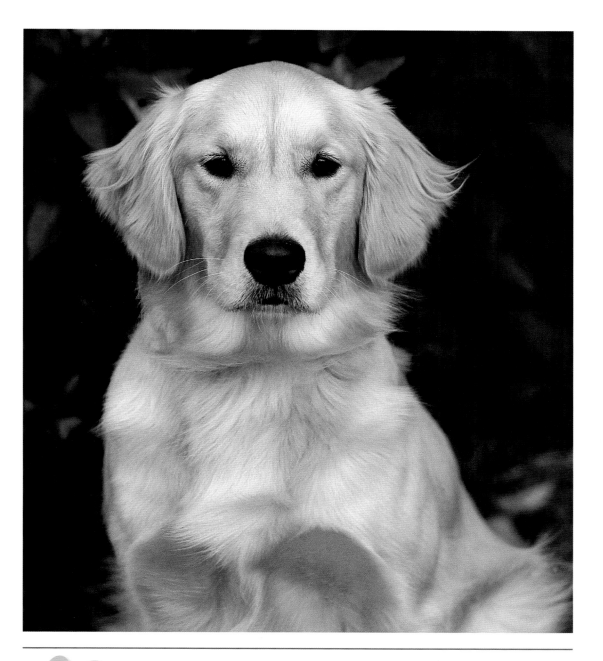

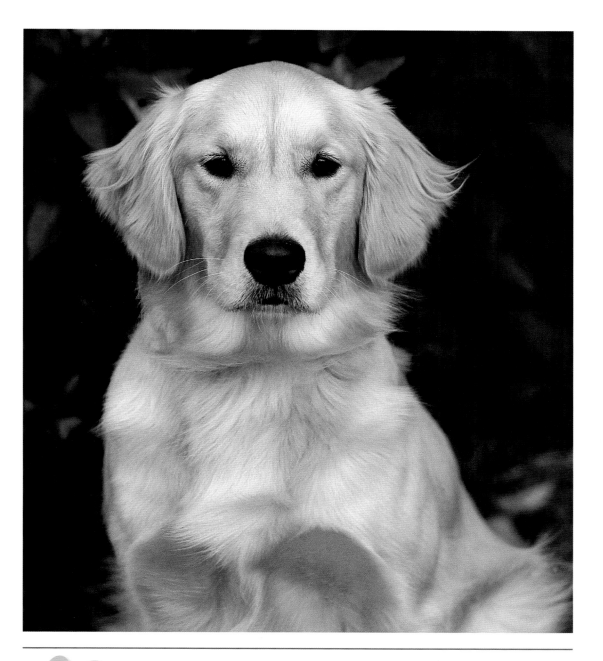

With the proper training, your Golden will be as well behaved as she is adorable. One certification that all dogs should receive is the American Kennel Club Canine Good Citizen, which rewards dogs with good manners. Go to **DogChannel.com/Club-Gold** and click on "Downloads" to get the 10 steps required for your dog to be a CGC.

JOIN OUR ONLINE
Club Gold™

is in position, then release him with a cue you will always use to tell him the stay is over. Common release cues are: "all done," "break," "free," "free dog," "at ease" and "OK."

▲ When your Golden will stay in a sit or down position while you click and treat, add your verbal stay cue. Say "stay," pause for a second or two, click and say "stay" again. Release.

▲ When your Golden Retriever is getting the idea, say "stay," whisk the treat out of sight behind your back, click the clicker and whisk the treat back. Be sure to get it all the way to his nose, so he doesn't jump up. Gradually increase the duration of the stay.

▲ When he will stay for 15 to 20 seconds, add small distractions: shuffling your feet, moving your arms, small hops. Gradually increase distractions. If your Golden makes mistakes, it means you're adding too much, too fast.

▲ When he'll stay for 15 to 20 seconds with distractions, gradually add distance. Have your Golden Retriever stay, take a half-step back, click, return and treat. When he'll stay with a half-step, tell him to stay, take a full step back, click and return. Always return to your dog to treat after you click, but

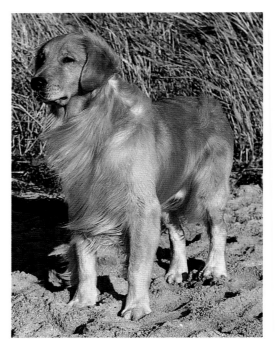

before you release. If you always return his stay becomes strong. If you call him to you, his stay gets weaker due to his eagerness to come to you.

COME: A reliable recall — coming when called — can be a challenging behavior to teach. It is possible, however. To succeed, you need to install an automatic response to your "come" cue — one so automatic that your Golden doesn't even stop to think when he hears it, but will spin on his heels and charge toward you at full speed.

▪ Start by charging a come cue the same way you charged your clicker. If your Golden already ignores the word "come," pick a different cue, like "front" or "hugs." Say your cue and feed him a bit of a scrumptious treat. Repeat this until his eyes light up when he hears the cue. Now you're ready to start training.

▪ With your Golden on a leash, run away several steps and cheerfully call out your charged cue. When he follows, click the

Behaviors are best trained by breaking them down into their simplest components, teaching those, and then linking them together to end up with the complete behavior. Keep treats small so you can reward many times without stuffing your retriever. Remember, don't bore your Golden; avoid excessive repetition.

it's a Fact

clicker. Feed him a treat when he reaches you. For a more enthusiastic come, run away at full speed as you call him. When he follows at a gallop, stop running, click and give him a treat. The better your Golden gets at coming, the farther away he can be when you call him.

■ Once your Golden Retriever understands the come cue, play with more people, each holding a clicker and treats. Stand a short distance apart and take turns calling and running away. Click and treat in turn as he comes to each of you. Gradually increase the distance until he comes flying to each person from a distance.

■ When you and your Golden are ready to practice in wide-open spaces, attach a long line — a 20- to 50-foot leash — to your dog, so you can get a hold of him if that taunting squirrel nearby is too much of a temptation. Then, head to a practice area where there are less tempting distractions.

HEEL: Heeling means that your dog can calmly walk beside you without pulling. It takes time and patience on your part to succeed at teaching your dog that you will not proceed unless he is walking beside you with ease. Pulling out ahead on the leash is definitely unacceptable.

● Begin by holding the leash in your left hand as your Golden sits beside your left leg. Move the loop end of the leash to your right hand but keep your left hand short on the leash so it keeps your dog close to you.

● Say "heel" and step forward on your left foot. Keep your Golden close to you and take three steps. Stop and have your dog sit next to you in what we now call the heel position. Praise verbally, but do not touch your dog. Hesitate a moment and begin again with "heel," taking three steps and stopping, at which point you tell your dog to sit again.

SMART TIP!

If you begin teaching the heel cue by taking long walks and letting your dog pull you along, she may misinterpret this action as acceptable. When you pull back on the leash to counteract her pulling, she will read that tug as a signal to pull even harder!

Your goal here is to have your dog walk those three steps without pulling on the leash. Once he will walk calmly beside you for three steps without pulling, increase the number of steps you take to five. When he will walk politely beside you while you take five steps, you can increase the length of your walk to 10 steps. Keep increasing the length of your stroll until your dog will walk beside you without pulling for as long as you want him to heel. When you stop heeling, indicate to your dog that the exercise is over by petting him and saying "OK, good dog." The "OK" is used as a release word, meaning that the exercise is finished and he is free to relax.

● If you are dealing with a Golden who insists on pulling you around, simply put on your brakes and stand your ground until your Golden realizes that the two of you are not going anywhere until he is beside you and moving at your pace, not his. It may take some time just standing there to convince your dog that you are the leader and you will be the one to decide on the direction and pace of your walk.

● Each time your dog looks up at you or slows down to give a slack leash between the two of you, quietly praise him and say, "Good heel. Good dog." Eventually, your Golden will begin to respond, and within a few days he will be walking politely beside you without pulling on the leash. At first, the training sessions should be kept short and very positive; soon your Golden Retriever will be able to walk nicely with you for increasingly longer distances. Remember to give your Golden Retriever free time and the opportunity to run and play when you have finished heel practice.

TRAINING TIPS

If not properly socialized and trained, even a well-bred Golden Retriever will exhibit bad behaviors such as jumping up, barking, chasing, chewing and other destructive behaviors. You can prevent these habits and help your Golden become the perfect dog you've wished for by following some basic training and behavior guidelines.

Be consistent. Consistency is important, not just in terms of what you allow your Golden to do (get on the sofa, perhaps) and not do (jump up on people), but also in the verbal and body language cues you use with your dog and in his daily routine.

Be gentle but firm. Positive training methods are very popular. Properly applied, dog-friendly methods are wonderfully ef-

fective, creating canine-human relationships based on respect and cooperation.

Manage behavior. All living things repeat behaviors that are rewarded. Behaviors that aren't reinforced will go away.

Provide adequate exercise. A tired Golden Retriever is a well-behaved Golden Retriever. Many behavior problems can be avoided, others resolved, by providing your Golden with enough exercise.

THE THREE-STEP PROGRAM

Perhaps it's too late to give your dog consistency, training and management from the start. Maybe he came from a Golden rescue shelter or you didn't realize the importance of these basic guidelines when he was a puppy. He already may have learned some bad behaviors. Perhaps they're even part of his genetic package. Many problems can be modified with ease using the following three-step process for changing an unwanted behavior.

Step No. 1: Visualize the behavior you want your dog to exhibit. If you simply try to stop your Golden from doing something, you leave a behavior vacuum. You must fill that vacuum with something, so your dog doesn't return to the same behavior or fill it with one that's even worse! If you're tired of your dog jumping up, decide what you'd prefer instead. A dog who greets people by sitting politely in front of them is a joy to own.

Step No. 2: Prevent your retriever from being rewarded for the behavior you don't want him to exhibit. Management to the rescue! When your Golden Retriever jumps up to greet you or get your attention, turn your back and step away to show him that jumping up on people no longer works in gaining their attention.

Step No. 3: Generously reinforce the desired behavior. Keep in mind that dogs will

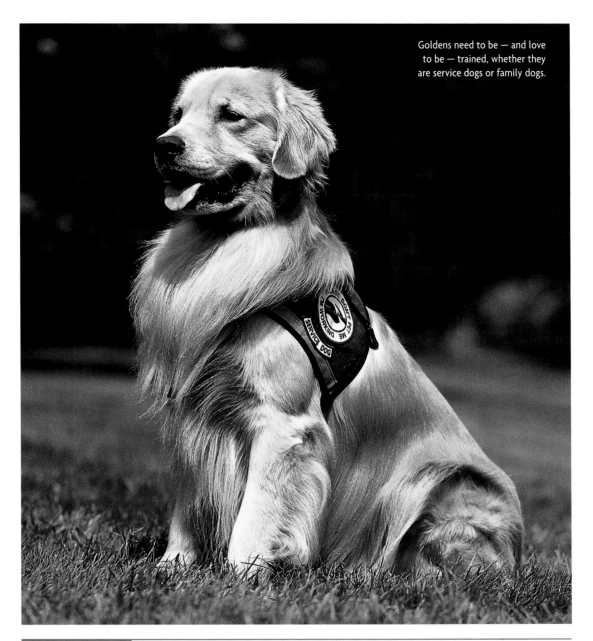

Goldens need to be — and love to be — trained, whether they are service dogs or family dogs.

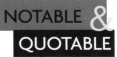
If you want to make your dog happy, create a digging spot where she's allowed to disrupt the earth. Encourage her to dig there by burying bones and toys and helping her dig them up. — Pat Miller, a certified dog trainer and owner of Peaceable Paws dog-training facility in Hagerstown, Md.

repeat behaviors that generate rewards. If your Golden no longer gets attention for jumping up and is heavily reinforced with attention and treats for sitting, he will offer sits instead of jumping, because he's learned that sitting will get him what he wants.

COUNTER-CONDITIONING

The three-step process helps to correct those behaviors that temporarily gives your Golden satisfaction. For example, he jumps up to get attention; he countersurfs because he finds good food on counters; he nips at your hands to get you to play with him.

The steps don't work well when you're dealing with behaviors that are based in strong emotion, such as aggression and fear, or with hardwired behaviors such as chasing prey. With these, you can change the emotional or hardwired response through counter-conditioning — programming a new emotional or automatic

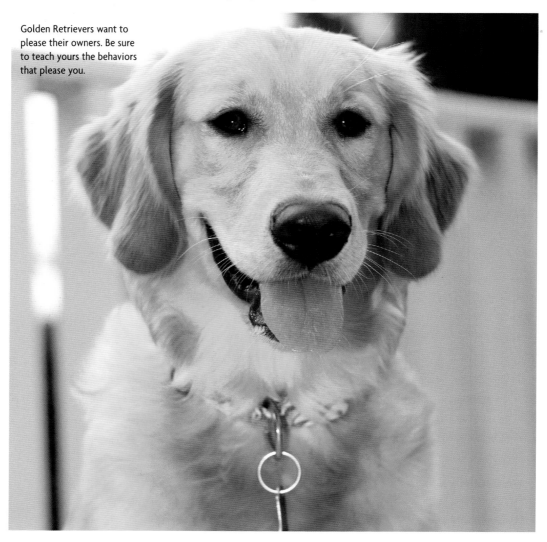

Golden Retrievers want to please their owners. Be sure to teach yours the behaviors that please you.

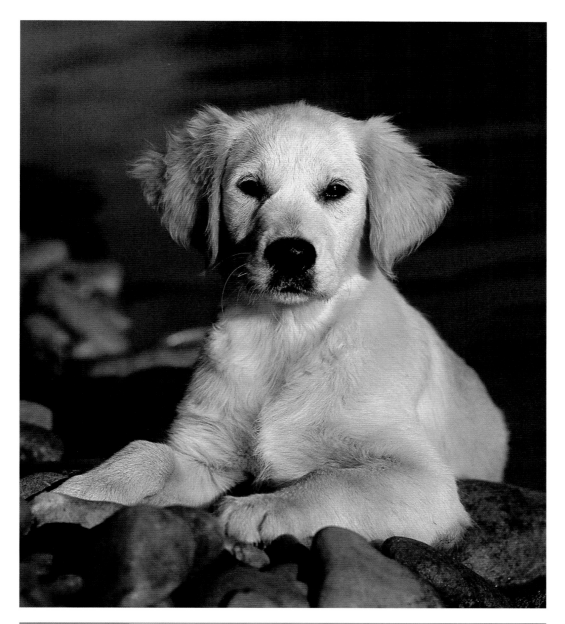

Be careful in the timing of your treats. A common mistake is to reward at the wrong time. If you reach in your pocket for a food treat and your dog gets up, do not give a treat. Otherwise, he will interpret your reaching in your pocket for complying with the stay cue. — Judy Super, a professional dog trainer in Minneapolis, Minn.

response to the stimulus by giving it a new association. Here's how you would counter condition a Golden Retriever who chases after skateboarders while you're walking him on a leash.

1. Have a large supply of high-value treats, such as canned chicken.

2. Station yourself with your Golden on a leash at a location where skateboarders will pass by at a subthreshold distance "X" — that is, where your Golden is alerted to the approaching person but doesn't bark.

3. Wait for a skateboarder. The instant your Golden notices the skateboarder, feed him bits of chicken, nonstop, until the skateboarder is gone. Stop feeding him.

4. Repeat many times until, when the skateboarder appears, your Golden looks at you with a big grin as if to say, "Yay! Where's my chicken?" This is a conditioned emotional response, or CER.

5. When you have a consistent CER at distance X, decrease the distance slightly, perhaps by one foot, and repeat until you consistently get the CER at this distance.

6. Continue decreasing the distance and obtaining a CER at each level, until a skateboarder zooming right past your Golden elicits the "Where's my chicken?" response. Now go back to distance X and add a second skateboarder. Continue this process of desensitization until your Golden Retriever doesn't turn a hair at a bevy of skateboarders.

LEAVE IT ALONE

Golden Retrievers enjoy eating, which makes it easy to train them using treats. But there's a downside to their gastronomic gusto — some Goldens will gobble down anything even remotely edible. This could include fresh food, rotten food, things that once were food and any item that's ever been in contact with food. So, if you don't want your Golden gulping trash, teach him to leave things alone when told.

Place a tempting tidbit on the floor and cover it with your hand (gloved against teeth, if necessary). Say your cue word ("leave it" or "nah"). Your dog might lick, nibble and paw your hand; don't give in, or you'll be rewarding bad manners.

Wait until he moves away, then click or praise and give a treat. Do not let your Golden Retriever eat the food that's on the floor, only the treats you give him. Repeat until your Golden stops moving toward the tempting food.

Lift your hand momentarily, letting your dog see the temptation. Say the cue word. Be ready to protect the treat but instantly reward him if he resists temptation. Repeat, moving your hand farther away and waiting longer before clicking and rewarding.

Increase the difficulty gradually — practice in different locations, add new temptations, drop treats from standing height, drop several at a time and step away.

Remember to use your cue word, so your dog will know what he's expected to do. Always reward good behavior! Rehearse this skill daily for a week. After that, you'll have enough real-life opportunities to practice.

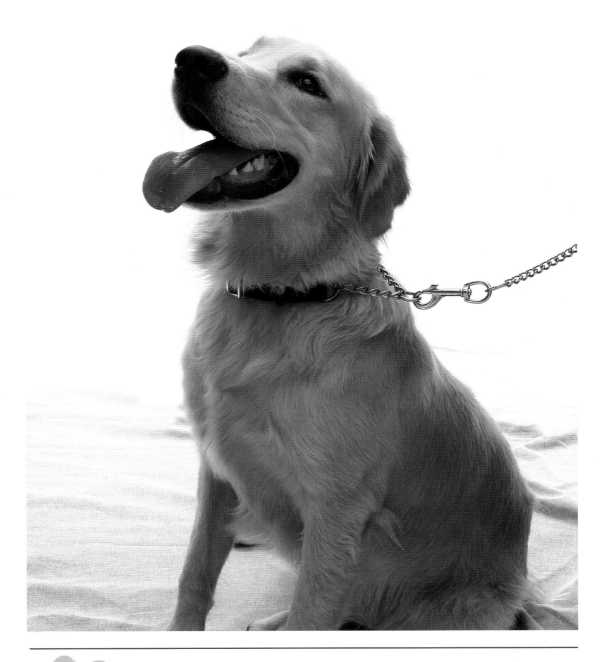

Even the best dogs have some bad habits. If you are frustrated with a particular behavior that your Golden exhibits, don't despair! Go online and join Club Gold, where you can ask other Golden owners for advice on dealing with excessive digging, stubbornness, housetraining issues and more. Log on to **DogChannel.com/Club-Gold** and click on "Community."

JOIN OUR ONLINE
Club Gold™

CHAPTER 11

CHANGING

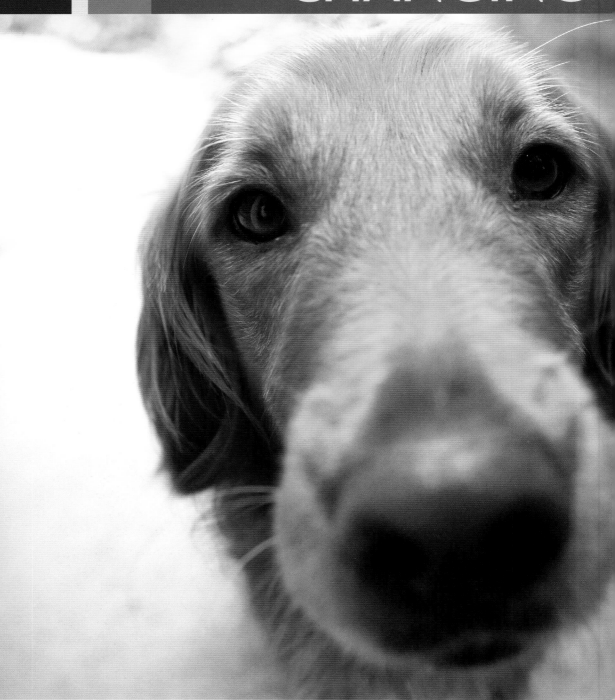

BAD BEHAVIOR

Discipline — training one to act in accordance with rules — brings order to life. It is as simple as that. Without discipline, particularly in a group society, chaos would ensue. Humans and canines are social animals and need some form of discipline in order to effectively function. Dogs need discipline in their lives in order to understand how their pack (you and other family members) functions and how they must act in order to survive.

Living with an untrained Golden Retriever is a lot like owning a piano that you do not know how to play; it is a nice object to look at but it does not do much more than that to bring you pleasure. Now, try taking piano lessons and suddenly the piano comes alive and brings forth magical sounds and rhythms that set your heart singing and your body swaying.

The same is true of your Golden Retriever. If your dog isn't trained, he may develop unacceptable behaviors that annoy you or cause family friction.

Did You Know?

Anxiety can make a pup miserable. Living in a world with scary, monsters and suspected retriever-eaters roaming the streets has to be pretty nerve-wracking. The good news is that timid dogs are not doomed to be forever ruled by fear. Owners who understand a timid Golden Retriever's needs can help her build self-confidence and a more optimistic view of life.

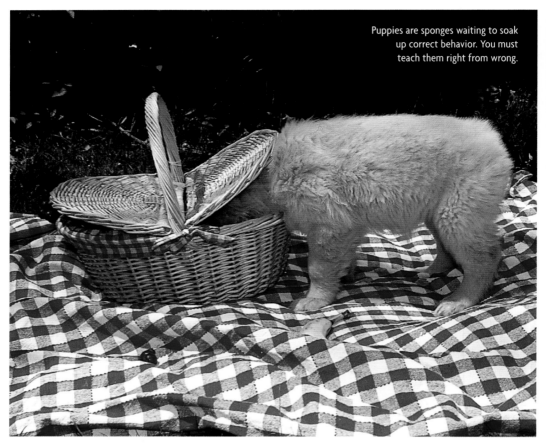

Puppies are sponges waiting to soak up correct behavior. You must teach them right from wrong.

To train your Golden, you can enroll in an obedience class to teach him good manners as you learn how and why he behaves the way he does. You will also find out how to communicate with your Golden and how to recognize and understand his communications with you. Suddenly your dog takes on a new role in your life; he is interesting, smart, well-behaved and fun to be with. He demonstrates his bond of devotion to you daily. In other words, your Golden Retriever does wonders for your ego because he constantly reminds you that you are not only his leader, you are his hero!

These classes teach dog obedience and counsel owners about their dogs' behavior have discovered interesting facts about dog ownership. For example, training dogs when they are puppies successfully develops well-mannered and well-adjusted

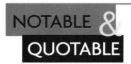

NOTABLE & QUOTABLE

The best way to get through to dogs is through their stomach and mind — not the use of force. You have to play a mind game with them.

— *Sara Gregware, a professional dog handler and trainer in Goshen, Conn.*

adults. Training an older Golden Retriever, from 6 months to 6 years, can produce almost equal results, providing that the owner accepts the dog's slower learning rate and is willing to patiently work to help him succeed. Unfortunately, many owners of untrained adult dogs lack the patience necessary, so they do not persist until their dogs are successful at learning particular behaviors.

Training a 10- to 16-week-old Golden pup (20 weeks maximum) is like working with a dry sponge in a pool of water. The pup soaks up whatever you teach him and constantly looks for more to do and learn. At this early age, his body is not yet producing hormones, and therein lies the reason for such a high success rate. Without hormones, he is focused on you and is not particularly interested in investigating other places, dogs, people, etc.

You are his leader; his provider of food, water, shelter and security. Your Golden latches onto you and wants to stay close. He usually will follow you from room to room, won't let you out of his sight when you are outdoors with him and will respond in like manner to the people and animals you encounter. If you greet a friend warmly, he will happily greet the person as well. If, however, you are hesitant, even anxious, about the approaching stranger, he will also respond accordingly.

Once your puppy begins to produce hormones, his natural curiosity emerges and he begins to investigate the world around him. It is at this time when you may notice your untrained dog begins to wander away and ignore your cues to stay close.

There are usually training classes within a reasonable distance of your home, but you also can do a lot to train your dog yourself. Sometimes classes are available but

SMART TIP!

The golden rule of dog training is simple. For each "question" (cue), there is only one correct answer (reaction). One cue equals one reaction. Keep practicing the cue until the dog reacts correctly without hesitation. Be repetitive but not monotonous. Dogs get bored just as people do; a bored dog's attention will not be focused on the lesson.

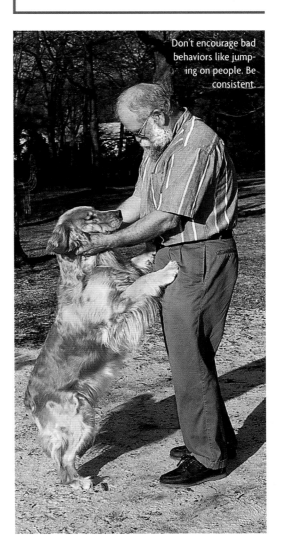

Don't encourage bad behaviors like jumping on people. Be consistent.

the tuition is too costly, whatever the circumstances, information about training your Golden Retriever without formal obedience classes lies within the pages of this book. If the recommended procedures are followed faithfully, you can expect positive results that will prove rewarding for both you and your dog.

Whether your new Golden Retriever is a puppy or a mature adult, the teaching methods and training techniques used in basic behaviors remain the same. No dog, whether puppy or adult, likes harsh or inhumane training methods. All creatures, however, respond favorably to gentle motivational methods and sincere praise and encouragement.

The following behavioral issues are those owners encounter the most. Keep in mind, however, that every dog and situation is unique. Because behavioral abnormalities are the leading reason for owners' abandoning their pets, we hope that you will make a valiant effort to solve your Golden Retriever's behavioral issues.

NIP NIPPING

As puppies start to teethe, they feel the need to sink their teeth into anything — unfortunately that includes your fingers, arms, hair, toes, whatever happens to be available. You may find this behavior cute for about the first five seconds — until you feel just how sharp those puppy teeth are.

Nipping is something you want to discourage immediately and consistently with a firm "No!" (or whatever number of firm "nos" it takes for your dog to understand that you mean business) and replace your finger with an appropriate chew toy.

STOP THAT WHINING

A puppy will often cry, whine, whimper, howl or make some type of commotion when he is left alone. This is basically his way of calling out for attention, to make sure you know he is there and that you have not forgotten about him. He feels insecure when he is left alone; for example, when you are out of the house and he is in his crate, or when you are in another part of the house and he cannot see you.

The noise he is making is an expression of the anxiety he feels for being left alone, so he needs to be taught that being alone is OK and normal. You are not actually training your Golden Retriever to stop making noise, you are training him to feel comfortable when he is alone and thus removing his need to make the noise.

This is where his crate with a cozy blanket and a toy comes in handy. When you want to know that your pup is safe when you are not there to supervise him, the best place for him to be is in his crate. In order for your pup to stay in his crate without making a fuss, he needs to be comfortable there. On that note, it is extremely important that the crate is never used as a form of punishment, or your Golden puppy will have a negative association with his crate.

Accustom your puppy to his crate in short, gradually increasing time intervals. During these periods, put him in the crate, maybe

Did You Know? Dogs do not understand our language. They can be trained, however, to react to a certain sound, at a certain volume. Never use your Golden Retriever's name during a reprimand, as she might begin to associate it with a bad thing!

Your Golden may howl, whine or otherwise vocalize her displeasure at your leaving the house and her being left alone. This is a normal case of separation anxiety, but there are things that can be done to eliminate this problem. Your dog needs to learn that she will be fine on her own for a while and that she will not wither away if she isn't attended to every minute of the day.

In fact, constant attention can lead to separation anxiety in the first place. If you are endlessly coddling and cuddling your Golden Retriever, she will come to expect this from you all of the time, and it will be more traumatic for her when you are not there.

To help minimize separation anxiety, make your entrances and exits as low-key as possible. Do not give your Golden a long, drawn-out goodbye, and do not smother her with hugs and kisses when you return. This will only make her miss you more when you are away. Another thing you can try is to give your dog a treat when you leave; this will keep her occupied, and off the fact that you just left and help her associate your leaving with a pleasant experience.

You may have to acclimate your Golden to being left alone in intervals, much like when you introduced her to her crate. Of course, when your dog starts whimpering as you approach the door, your first instinct will be to run to her and comfort her, but don't do it! Eventually, she will adjust and be just fine — if you take it in small steps. Her anxiety stems from being placed in an unfamiliar situation; by familiarizing her with being alone, she will learn that she will be just fine.

When your Golden Retriever is alone in the house, confine her in her crate or a designated dog-proof area. This should be the area in which she sleeps, so she will already feel comfortable there. This should make her feel more at ease for those times she is left alone.

This is just one of the many examples in which a crate is an invaluable tool for you and your Golden Retriever, and another reinforcement of why your dog should view her crate as a happy place of her own.

with a treat, and stay in the room with him. If he cries or makes a fuss, do not go to him, but stay in his sight. Gradually, he will realize staying in his crate is all right without your help and it will not be so traumatic for him when you are not around. You may want to leave the radio on softly when you leave the house; the sound of human voices can comfort him.

CHEW ON THIS

The national canine pastime is chewing! Every dog loves to sink his "canines" into a tasty bone, but anything will do! Dogs chew to massage their gums, make their new teeth feel better and exercise their jaws. This is a natural behavior deeply embedded in all things canine. Owners should not stop their dog's chewing, but redirect it to chew-worthy objects. A smart owner will purchase proper chew toys for their Golden Retriever, like strong nylon bones made for large dogs. Be sure that these devices are safe and durable because your dog's safety is at risk.

The best solution is prevention: Put your shoes, handbags and other alluring objects in their proper places (out of the reach of the growing canine mouth). Direct puppies to their toys whenever you see them tasting the furniture legs or the leg of your pants. Make a loud noise to attract your Golden Retriever pup's attention and immediately escort him to his chew toy and engage him with the toy for at least four minutes, praising and encouraging him all the while.

NO MORE JUMPING

Jumping is a dog's friendly way of saying hello! Some owners don't mind when their dog jumps, which is fine for them. The problem arises when guests arrive and the dog greets them in the same manner — whether they like it or not! However friendly the greeting may be, chances are your visitors will not appreciate your dog's enthusiasm. Your dog will not be able to distinguish upon whom he can jump and whom he cannot. Therefore, it is probably best to discourage this behavior entirely.

Pick a cue such as "off" (avoid using "down" because you will use that for your dog to lie down) and tell him "off" when he jumps. Place him on the ground on all fours and have him sit, praising him the whole time. Always lavish him with praise and petting when he is in the sit position, that way you are still giving him a warm, affectionate greeting, because you are as pleased to see him as he is to see you!

UNWANTED BARKING MUST GO

Barking is how dogs talk. It can be somewhat frustrating because it is not easy to tell what your dog means by his bark: is he excited, happy, frightened, angry? Whatever it is your dog is trying to say, he should not be punished for barking. It is only when barking becomes excessive, and when excessive barking becomes a bad habit, that the behavior needs to be modified.

If an intruder came into your home in the middle of the night and your dog barked a warning, wouldn't you be pleased? You would probably deem your dog a hero, a wonderful guardian and protector of the

SMART TIP!

Do not carry your puppy to her potty area. Lead her there on a leash or, better yet, encourage her to follow you to the spot. If you start carrying her, you might end up doing this routine for a long time, and your puppy will have the satisfaction of having trained you.

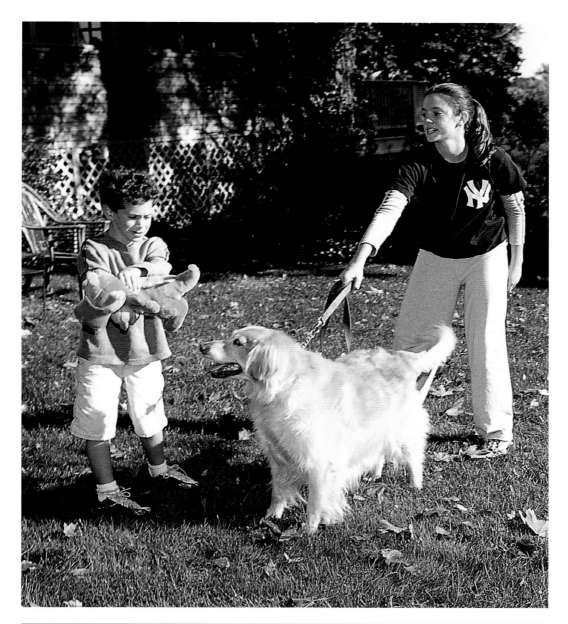

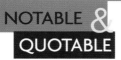

NOTABLE & QUOTABLE *Stage false departures. Pick up your car keys and put on your coat, then put them away and go about your routine. Do this several times a day, ignoring your dog while you do it. Soon, her reaction to these triggers will decrease.*

— September Morn, a dog trainer and behavior specialist in Bellingham, Wash.

home. On the other hand, if a friend unexpectedly drops by, rings the doorbell and is greeted with a sudden sharp bark, you probably would be annoyed at your dog. But isn't it the same behavior? Your dog doesn't know any better … unless he sees who is at the door and it is someone he is familiar with, he will bark as a means of vocalizing that his (and your) territory is being threatened. While your friend is not posing a threat, it is all the same to your dog. Barking is his means of letting you know there is an intruder, whether friend or foe, on your property. This type of barking is instinctive and should not be discouraged.

Excessive, habitual barking, however, is a problem that should be corrected early on. As your Golden Retriever grows up, you will be able to tell when his barking is purposeful and when it is for no reason, you will able to distinguish your dog's different barks and with what they are associated. For example,

the bark when someone comes to the door will be different from the bark when he is excited to see you. It is similar to a person's tone of voice, except that your Golden has to completely rely on tone because he does not have the benefit of using words. An incessant barker will be evident at an early age.

There are some things that encourage barking. For example, if your dog barks nonstop for a few minutes and you give him a treat to quiet him, he believes you are rewarding him for barking. He will now associate barking with getting a treat, and will keep barking until he receives his reward.

FOOD STEALING AND BEGGING

Is your Golden Retriever devising ways of stealing food from your cupboards? If so, you must answer the following questions: Is your dog really hungry? Why is there food on the coffee table? Face it, some dogs are more

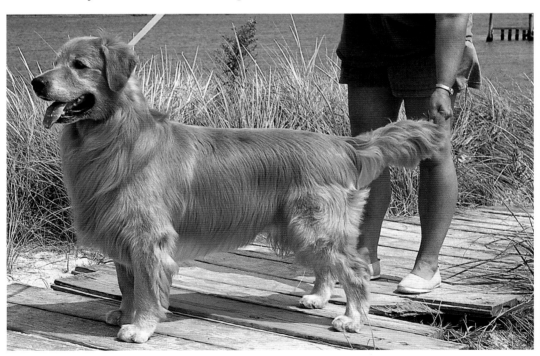

food motivated than others; some are totally obsessed by a slab of brisket and can only think of their next meal. Food stealing is terrific fun and always yields a great reward — food, glorious food!

Therefore, the owner's goal is to make the reward less rewarding, even startling! Plant a shaker can (an empty can with a lid and filled with coins) on the table so that it catches your Golden off-guard. There are other devices available that will surprise your dog when he is looking for a mid-afternoon snack. Such remote-control devices, though not the first choice of some trainers, allow the correction to come from the object instead of you. These devices are also useful to keep your snacking Golden from napping on forbidden furniture.

Just like food stealing, begging is a favorite pastime of hungry pups with the same reward — food! Dogs learn quickly that humans love that feed-me pose and that their owners keep the good food for themselves. Why would humans dine on kibble when they can cook up sausages and kielbasa? Begging is a conditioned response related to a specific stimulus, time and place; the sounds of the kitchen, cans and bottles opening, crinkling bags and the smell of food preparation will excite your chowhound and soon his paws will be in the air!

Here is how to stop this behavior: Never give in to a beggar, no matter how appealing or desperate! By giving in, you are rewarding your dog for jumping up, whining and rubbing his nose into you. By ignoring your dog, you eventually will force the behavior into extinction. Note that his behavior will likely get worse before it disappears, so be sure there are not any "softies" in the family who will give in to your Golden Retriever every time he whimpers "Please."

DIG THIS

Digging, seen as a destructive behavior by humans, is actually quite a natural behavior in dogs. Their desire to dig can be irrepressible and most frustrating. When digging happens, it is an innate behavior redirected into something the dog can do in his everyday life. In the wild, a dog would be actively seeking food, making his own shelter, etc. He would be using his paws in a purposeful manner for his survival. Because you provide him with food and shelter, he has no need to use his paws for these purposes and so the energy he would be using may manifest itself in the form of holes all over your yard and flower beds.

Perhaps your dog is digging as a reaction to boredom — it is somewhat similar to someone eating a whole bag of chips in front of the TV — because they are there and there is nothing better to do! Basically, the answer is to provide your dog with adequate play and exercise so his mind and paws are occupied, and so he feels as if he is doing something useful.

Of course, digging is easiest to control if it is stopped as soon as possible, but it is often hard to catch your dog in the act. If your

Do not have long practice sessions with your Golden. She will easily become bored if you do. Also: Never practice when you are tired, ill, worried or in a negative mood. This will transmit to your retriever and may have an adverse effect on her performance.

Golden Retriever is a compulsive digger and is not easily distracted by other activities, you can designate an area on your property where it is OK for him to dig. If you catch him digging in an off-limits area of the yard, immediately bring him to the approved area and praise him for digging there. Keep a close eye on him so you can catch him in the act — that is the only way to make him understand where digging is permitted and where it is not. If you take him to a hole he dug an hour ago and tell him "no," he will understand that you are not fond of holes, dirt or flowers. If you catch him while he is stifle-deep in your tulips, that is when he will get your message.

POOP ALERT!

Humans find feces eating, aka *coprophagia*, one of the most disgusting behaviors that their dog could engage in; yet to your dog it is perfectly normal. Vets have found that diets with low digestibility, containing relatively low levels of fiber and high levels of starch, increase *coprophagia*. Therefore, high-fiber diets may decrease the likelihood of coprophagia. To discourage this behavior, feed complete and balanced food. If changes in his diet don't work, and no medical cause can be found, you will have to modify his behavior through environmental control before it becomes a habit.

There are some tricks you can try, such as adding an unpleasant-tasting substance to the feces to make them unpalatable or adding something to your dog's food which will make it unpleasant tasting after it passes through your dog. The best way to prevent your dog from eating his stool is to make it unavailable — clean up after he eliminates and remove any stool from the yard. If it is not there, he cannot eat it.

Never reprimand your dog for stool eating, as this rarely impresses your dog. Vets recommend distracting your Golden Retriever while he is in the act. Another option is to muzzle your dog when he goes in the yard to relieve himself; this usually is effective within 30 to 60 days. *Coprophagia* is mostly seen in pups 6 to 12 months, and usually disappears around the dog's first birthday.

AGGRESSION

Aggression, when not controlled, always becomes dangerous. An aggressive Golden Retriever, no matter his size, may lunge at, bite or even attack a person or another dog. Aggressive behavior is not to be tolerated. It is more than just inappropriate behavior; it is unsafe. It is painful for a family to watch their dog become unpredictable in his behavior to the point where they are afraid of him. While not all aggressive behavior is dangerous, growling and baring teeth can be frightening. It is important to ascertain why your dog is acting in this manner. Aggression is a display of dominance, and your dog should not have the dominant role in his pack, which is, in this case, your family.

It is important not to challenge an aggressive dog, as this could provoke an attack. Observe your Golden Retriever's body language. Does he make direct eye contact and stare? Does he try to make himself as large as possible: ears pricked, chest

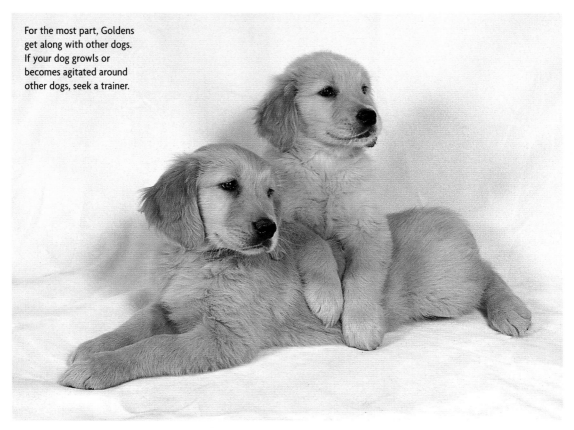

For the most part, Goldens get along with other dogs. If your dog growls or becomes agitated around other dogs, seek a trainer.

out, neck arched? Height and size signify authority in a dog pack — being taller or "above" another dog literally means that he is "above" in the social status. These body signals tell you that your Golden Retriever thinks he is in charge, a problem that needs to be addressed. An aggressive dog is unpredictable: You never know when he is going to strike and what he is going to do. You cannot understand why a dog who is playful and loving one minute is growling and snapping the next.

The best solution is to consult a behavioral specialist, one who has experience with Golden Retrievers if possible. Together, perhaps you can pinpoint the cause of your dog's aggression and do something about it. An aggressive dog cannot be trusted and a dog who cannot be trusted is not safe to have as a family pet. If, very unusually, you find that your dog has become untrustworthy and you feel it necessary to seek a new home with a more suitable family and environment, explain fully to the new owners all

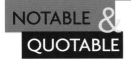

The purpose of puppy classes is for puppies to learn how to learn. The pups get the training along the way, but the training is almost secondary.

— *professional trainer Peggy Shunick Duezabou of Helena, Mont.*

your reasons for rehoming the dog to be fair to all who are concerned. In the very worst case, you will have to consider euthanasia.

AGGRESSION TOWARD DOGS

A dog's aggressive behavior toward another dog sometimes stems from insufficient exposure to other dogs at an early age. It is the breeder and owner's responsibility to curb and redirect any signs of aggression so that your Golden Retriever can become an upright member of canine society. If other dogs make your Golden nervous and agitated, he might use aggression as a defense mechanism. A dog who has not received sufficient exposure to other canines tends to believe he is the only dog on the planet. He becomes so dominant

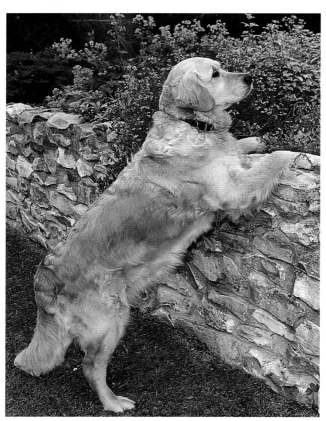

that he does not even show signs that he is fearful or threatened. Without growling or any other signal as a warning, he will lunge at and bite another dog. A way to correct this is to let your Golden Retriever approach another dog only when walking on a leash. Watch very closely and at the first sign of aggression, correct your dog and pull him away. Scold him for any sign of discomfort, and praise him when he ignores or tolerates the other dog. Keep this up until he stops the aggressive behavior, learns to ignore other dogs or accepts other dogs. Praise him lavishly for his correct behavior.

DOMINANT AGGRESSION

A social hierarchy is firmly established in a wild dog pack; dogs want to dominate those under them and please those above them. They know there must be a leader. If you are not the obvious choice for emperor, your dog will assume the throne! These conflicting, innate desires are what you are up against when training your dog. In training a dog to obey cues, you are reinforcing the fact that you are the top dog in the "pack" and that your dog should, and should want to, serve his superior. Thus, you are suppressing your dog's urge to dominate by correcting his behavior and making him obedient.

An important part of training is taking every opportunity to reinforce that you are the leader. The simple action of making your Golden Retriever sit to wait for his food says you control when he eats, and that he is dependent on you for food. Although it may be difficult, do not give in to your dog's wishes every time he whines at you or looks at you with his pleading eyes. It requires constant effort to show your dog that his place in the pack is at the bottom.

This is not meant to sound cruel or inhumane. After all, you love your Golden, and you should treat him with care and affection. You certainly did not get a dog just so you could boss around another creature. Dog training is not about being cruel or feeling important, it is about molding your dog's behavior into what is acceptable and teaching him to live by your rules. In theory, it is quite simple: catch him displaying appropriate behavior, and reward him for it. Add a dog into the equation, and it becomes a bit more trying and challenging, but as a rule of thumb, positive reinforcement works best.

With a dominant dog, punishment and negative reinforcement can have the opposite effect of what you are trying to achieve. It can make your dog fearful and/or act out aggressively if he feels he is being challenged. Remember, a dominant dog perceives himself at the top of the social heap and will fight to defend his perceived status. The best way to prevent that is to never give him reason to think he is in control in the first place. If you are having trouble training your Golden Retriever, and it seems as if he is constantly challenging your authority, seek the help of an obedience trainer or behavioral specialist. A professional will work with both you and your dog to teach you effective techniques to use at home. Beware of trainers who rely on excessively harsh methods; scolding is necessary now and then, but the focus in your training should always be positive reinforcement.

If you can isolate what brings out your Golden's fear reaction, you can help him get over it. Supervise your Golden Retriever's interactions with people and other dogs, and praise him when it goes well. If he starts to act aggressively in a situation, correct him and remove him from the situation. Do not let people approach your dog and start petting him without your expressed permission. That way, you can have your dog sit to accept petting and praise him when he behaves appropriately; you are focusing on praise and modifying his behavior by rewarding him. By being gentle and by supervising his interactions, you are showing him that there is no need to be afraid or defensive.

SEXUAL BEHAVIOR

Dogs exhibit certain sexual behaviors that may have influenced your choice of selecting a male or female when you first purchased your Golden Retriever. To a certain extent, spaying/neutering will eliminate these behaviors, but if you are purchasing a dog whom you wish to breed, you should be aware of what you will have to deal with throughout your dog's life.

Female dogs usually have two estruses (heat cycles) per year with each season lasting about three weeks. These are the only times in which a female dog will mate, and she usually will not allow this until the second week of the cycle, but this does vary from female to female. If not bred during the heat cycle, it is not uncommon for a female to experience a false pregnancy, in which her mammary glands swell and she exhibits maternal tendencies toward toys or other objects.

Smart Golden Retriever owners must also recognize that mounting is not merely a form of sexual expression; it is also one of dominance. Be consistent and persistent in your training your dog, and you will find that you can "move mounters."

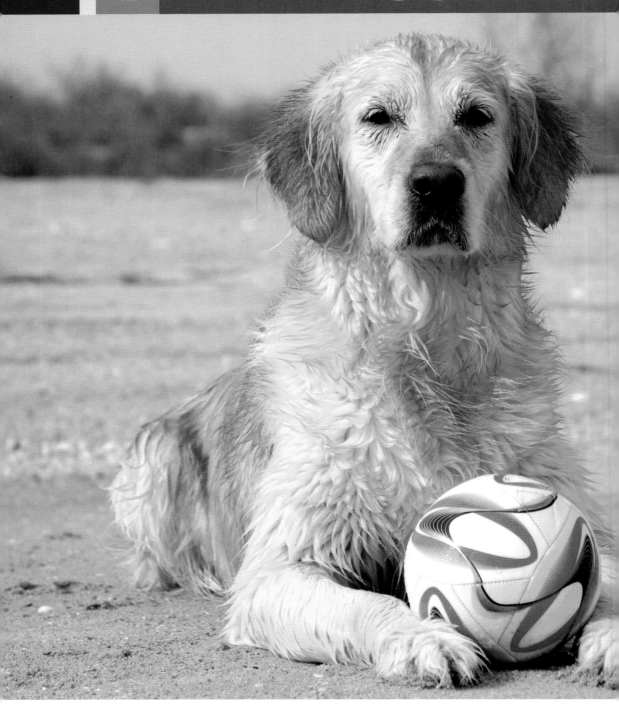

GAMES

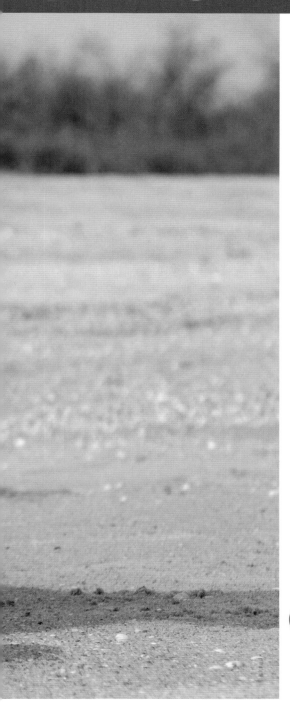

One of the best ways to nurture a cooperative and solid relationship with your Golden Retriever is to become involved in an activity both of you can enjoy. A bored Golden can easily become a troublesome dog.

Deciding what recreational activity you and your Golden would enjoy the most takes some consideration. Do you want a sport, such as agility, where you and your dog are both active participants? Would you prefer an activity, such as flyball, where your dog does most of the running? Does something less physical, such as visiting senior citizens, sound more like your cup of tea? Perhaps a brief synopsis of some of the more popular dog-friendly recreations will help you narrow down the choices.

EXERCISE OPTIONS

All Golden Retrievers need exercise to keep them physically and mentally healthy. An inactive dog is an overweight dog, who will likely suffer joint strain or torn ligaments. Inactive dogs also are prone to mischief and may do anything to relieve their boredom. This often leads to behavioral problems, such as chewing or barking. Regular daily exercise, such as walks and play sessions, will keep your Golden slim, trim and happy.

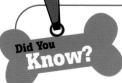

Did You Know?

The Fédération Internationale Cynologique is the world kennel club that governs dog shows in Europe and elsewhere around the world.

SMART TIP!

Before You Begin

Because of the physical demands of sporting activities, a Golden puppy shouldn't begin official training until she is done growing. That doesn't mean, though, that you can't begin socializing her to sports. Talk to your veterinarian about what age is appropriate to begin.

Provide your Golden with interactive play that stimulates his mind as well as his body. It's a good idea to have a daily period of one-on-one play, especially with a puppy or young dog. Continue this type of interaction throughout your dog's life, and you will build a lasting bond. Even senior Golden Retrievers need the stimulation that activity provides.

If your Golden is older or overweight, consult with your veterinarian to determine about how much and what type of exercise he needs. Usually, a 10- to 15-minute walk once a day is a good start. As the pounds start to drop off, your dog's energy level will rise, and you can increase the amount of daily exercise.

Whether a dog is trained in the structured environment of a class or alone with his owner at home, there also are many sporting activities that can bring fun and rewards to dog and owner once they have mastered basic training techniques.

AGILITY TRIALS

Agility is a fast-growing sport, attracting dogs of all kinds and their equally diverse owners. In agility, the dog is off leash, is guided by the handler and runs a course of

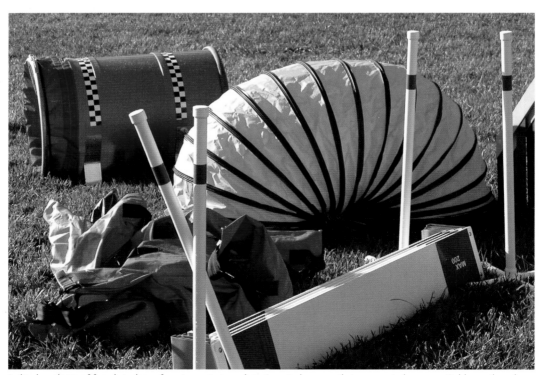

Agility has plenty of fun obstacles — from jumps to tunnels to turns to hoops — that are sure to keep your Golden enthused.

obstacles including jumps, tunnels, A-frames, elevated boards called dog walks and others. Basically, the dog must navigate through obstacles in proper order and style within a set time. As in obedience, the team can strive for high honors, the titles only or simply the joy of working together.

Most training facilities require that dogs have some basic obedience before entering an agility class because your dog must be responsive to you and reliable about not interfering with other dogs and handlers or running off. It is also important to allow your puppy to mature before undertaking agility's jumps and sharp turns because young bones and joints are injured more easily than mature ones.

Again, multiple organizations sponsor agility titles at all levels, from novice through advanced. The rules, procedures and obstacles vary somewhat among the organizations, so, again, it's important to obtain and read the appropriate rule book before entering your dog in competition. In addition to the American Kennel Club and the United Kennel Club, the United States Dog Agility Association and the North American Dog Agility Council also offer agility trials and titles. (Turn to the Resources chapter on page 166 for contact information).

The AKC offers Novice Agility, Open Agility, Agility Excellent and Master Agility Excellent titles. To achieve an MX title, a dog must first earn the AX title, then earn qualifying scores in the agility excellent class at 10 licensed or member agility trials.

The USDAA offers eight agility titles. An Agility Dog has achieved three clear rounds (no faults) under two different judges in the starters or novice category of competition. An Advanced Agility Dog has achieved three clear rounds under two different judges in the Advanced class. The Masters Agility Dog has demonstrated versatility by achieving three clear rounds under two different judges in the masters standard agility class.

In addition, a dog must receive a qualifying score at the masters level in each of the following: Gamblers Competition, to demonstrate proficiency in distance control and handling; Pairs or Team Relay, to demonstrate cooperative team effort and good sportsmanship; Jumping Class, to demonstrate a dog's jumping ability and fluid working habit; and Snooker Competition, to further demonstrate a dog and handler's versatility in strategic planning. To earn a Jumpers Master, Gamblers Master, Snooker Master or Relay Master title, a dog must achieve five clear rounds in the appropriate class. A USDAA Agility Dog Champion has earned the MAD, SM, GM, JM and RM titles. The USDAA also recognizes the Agility Top 10 annually.

USDAA promotes competition by hosting major tournament events, including its Grand Prix of Dog Agility championships. The Dog Agility Masters Team Pentathlon

---

NOTABLE & QUOTABLE

The Golden Retriever, though often thought of as a great family dog, is an active dog who was bred to do a job. Most people who fall in love with their neighbor's Golden don't know this, and often are very surprised at the amount of energy and mischief they can get into, especially as puppies and adolescent dogs.

— trainer Gerilyn Bielakiewicz of Malden, Mass.

Championship promotes agility as a team sport, and the Dog Agility Steeplechase championship focuses on speed performance. Dogs must be registered with the USDAA in order to compete in its events.

The USDAA also offers programs for older dogs as well as younger handlers. The Veterans Program is for dogs 7 years of age or older. The Junior Handler Program is for handlers up to 18 years of age and is designed to encourage young people to participate in dog agility as a fun, recreational family sport.

The North American Dog Agility Council offers certificates of achievement for the regular, jumpers and gamblers classes. The purpose of the regular agility class is to demonstrate the handler and dog's ability to perform all of the agility obstacles safely and at a moderate rate of speed. At the open level, the goal is to test the handler and dog's ability to perform the obstacles more quickly and with more directional and distance control and obstacle discrimination.

At the elite level, more complex handler strategies are tested, with the dog moving at a brisk pace. The dog may be entered in the standard, veterans or junior handlers division. In all divisions, certification in the regular agility classes will require three qualifying rounds under at least two different judges. NADAC also awards the Agility Trial Champion title.

OBEDIENCE TRIALS

Obedience trials in the United States trace back to the early 1930s, when organized obedience training was developed to demonstrate how well dogs and their owners could work together. Helen Whitehouse Walker, a Standard Poodle fancier, pioneered obedience trials after she modeled a series of exercises after the Associated Sheep, Police and Army Dog Society of Great Britain. Since Walker initiated the first trials, competitive obedience has grown by leaps and bounds, and today more than 2,000 trials are held in the United States every year, with more than 100,000 dogs competing. Any registered AKC or UKC dog can enter an obedience trial for the club in which he is registered, regardless of conformational disqualifications or neutering.

Obedience trials are divided into three levels of progressive difficulty. At the first level, Novice, the dogs compete for the title of Companion Dog; at the intermediate level, Open, dogs compete for a Companion Dog Excellent title; and at the Advanced level, dogs compete for a Utility Dog title. Classes are subdivided into "A" (for beginners) and "B" (for more experienced handlers). A perfect score at any level is 200, and a dog must score 170 or better to earn a "leg," three of which are needed to earn the title. To earn points, the dog must score more than 50 percent of the available points in each exercise; the possible points range from 20 to 40.

Once a dog has earned the Utility Dog title, he can compete with other proven obedience dogs for the coveted title of Utility Dog Excellent, which requires that the dog win "legs" in 10 shows. In 1977, the title Obedience Trial Champion was established by the AKC. Utility Dogs who earn legs in Open B and Utility B earn points toward their Obedience Trial Champion title. To become an OTCh., a dog needs to earn 100 points, which requires three first place wins in Open B and Utility B under three different judges.

The Grand Prix of obedience trials, the AKC National Obedience Invitational, gives qualifying Utility Dogs the chance to win the newest and highest title: National Obedience Champion. Only the top 25 ranked obedience dogs, plus any dog ranked in the top three in his breed, are allowed to compete.

RALLY BEHIND RALLY

Rally is a sport that combines competitive obedience with elements of agility but which is less demanding than either one of these activities. Rally was designed keeping the average dog owner in mind and is easier than many other sporting activities.

At a rally event, dogs and handlers are asked to move through 10 to 20 different stations, depending on the level of competition. The stations are marked by numbered signs, which tell the handler the exercise to be performed. The exercises vary from making different types of turns to changing pace.

Dogs can earn rally titles as they get better at the sport and move through the different levels. The titles to strive for are Rally Novice, Rally Advanced, Rally Excellent and Rally Advanced Excellent.

To get your Golden Retriever puppy prepared to enter a rally competition, focus on teaching him basic obedience, for starters. Your dog must know the five basic obedience cues — sit, down, stay, come and heel — and perform them well. Next, you can enroll your dog in a rally class. Although he must be at least 6 months of age to compete in rally, you can start training long before his 6-month birthday.

HUNTING COMPANIONS

The Golden Retriever was developed, of course, to retrieve waterfowl and upland game birds, and the breed still excels as a top-notch hunting companion. Fortunately for owners who don't want to hunt, hunting tests and field trials are available to test the Golden's retrieving abilities. Once again,

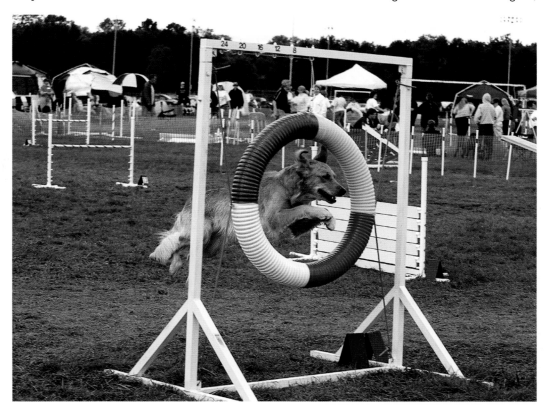

If you find your Golden isn't suited for group activities, once you get your veterinarian's OK and basic obedience training behind you, you and your retriever can find plenty of opportunities for exercise, training and strengthening the bond between you two right in your own backyard.

even if you decide not to pursue titles, it is thrilling to watch a dog doing what he was meant to do.

The Golden Retriever Club of America offers a Working Certificate and a Working Certificate Excellent. The WC is meant to encourage all owners of Goldens to maintain the natural hunting and retrieving abilities that are considered genetically vital to the breed. The WC test requires a dog to complete land and water tests, using ducks, game birds or pigeons. According to the GRCA, "the tests are designed to demonstrate the following natural abilities of a retriever as stated in the AKC Retriever Advisory Committee Supplement: accurate marking and memory of falls, intelligence, attention, style, good nose, perseverance, desire and trainability." The WCX is intended to encourage the development of natural hunting and retrieving abilities through training.

The AKC offers hunt tests and field trials for AKC-registered Goldens. A Junior Hunter title is awarded to a dog who has acquired qualifying scores in the Junior Hunting test at four AKC-licensed or member club hunting tests. A Senior Hunter title is awarded when the dog has acquired qualifying scores in the Senior Hunting test at five hunting tests. A Master Hunter title is earned by acquiring qualifying scores in the Master Hunting test at six hunting tests. The AKC also offers a Field Champion and Amateur Field Champion title. A dog who earns both an FC title and a show Champion title is designated a Dual Champion. If the dog also earns an Obedience Championship title, he is a Triple Champion.

The Hunting Retriever Club, affiliated with the UKC, offers hunting tests in which dogs earn points toward titles awarded by the UKC. Titles offered in the Hunting Retriever Club program are Started Hunting Retriever, Hunting Retriever, Hunting Retriever Champion, Grand Hunting Retriever Champion and Upland Hunting Retriever.

The North American Hunting Retriever Association helps clubs organize throughout North America to educate the public in the use of purebred hunting retrievers as conservation animals and to promote the field testing of retrievers in simulated hunting situations. NAHRA tests are not competitive. Instead, each dog competes against a performance standard. To be designated a Started Retriever, the dog must qualify four times in the started testing category. For the Working Retriever title, the dog must earn 20 points in the intermediate testing category. Master Hunting Retriever is awarded to a dog that qualifies either five times in the senior testing category or four times in the senior testing category if the dog has a WR title. Grand Master Hunting Retriever is awarded to a dog that qualifies 15 times in the senior testing category. Other NAHRA awards and events include the Brass Band Award and the NAHRA Invitational Field Test.

If you are interested in training your Golden for fieldwork and maybe even participating in hunt tests or trials, contact your nearest Golden Retriever club for information. Many clubs hold training meetings or have a number of members who are actively training for field events. Wear clothes that you can get wet and mucky, and have a good time; your Golden surely will!

TRACKING TALES

Tracking, by nature, is a vigorous, non-competitive outdoor sport. The AKC awards titles for registered dogs trained to track, but even if you don't want to pursue a title, training your Golden to track can be great fun, providing exercise for you and your dog and giving you the opportunity to observe the incredible powers of the canine nose. Golden Retrievers have good, busy noses — as you know if you've ever taken one for a walk. You may as well put that talent to use! The best way to train is with other people

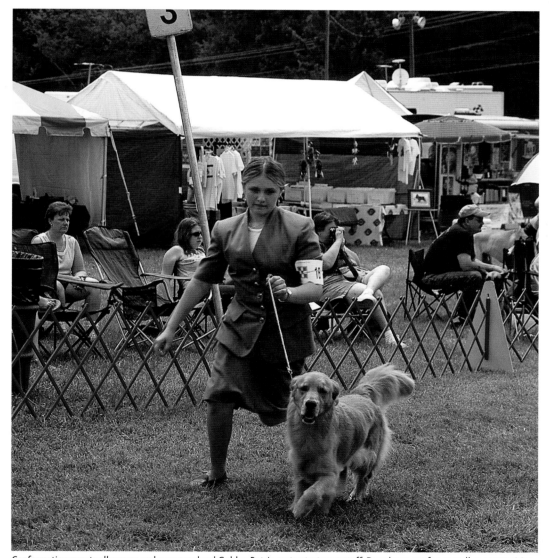

Conformation events allow you and your purebred Golden Retriever to strut your stuff. Dog shows are fun as well as competitive.

Teaching your Golden Retriever to watch your every move begins when you first bring her home. Puppies will automatically follow you, even without a leash, because they want to be with you, especially if you have a treat in your hand. Keep your dog on your left side and offer her a small piece of food with each step you take. In no time, your Golden Retriever pup will think that you're an automatic treat dispenser, and she will never leave your side.

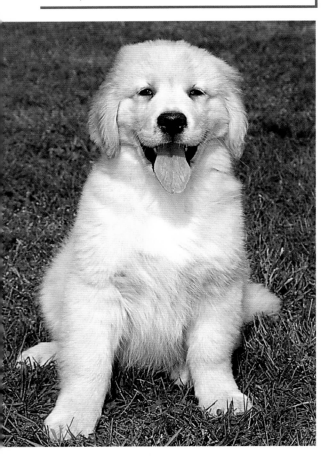

and their dogs; if you can find a tracking club, all the better. Some obedience clubs also have groups of people interested in training their dogs to track.

The purpose of a tracking test is to demonstrate the dog's ability to recognize and follow human scent. Before a dog is permitted to enter a tracking test, his handler must obtain a written statement certifying that the dog has satisfactorily performed a certification test within one year of the date the test is to be held. The statement must be signed by a person approved by the AKC to judge tracking tests. The certification test should be of a complexity equivalent to the tracking test and take place under conditions similar to such a test.

A Tracking Dog title is given to a dog who has been certified by two judges to have passed a licensed or member club tracking test. To earn a TD, the dog must track a person 440 to 500 yards away with three to five changes of direction. The track is laid 30 minutes to two hours before the dog begins scenting.

A Tracking Dog Excellent title requires two passes of the Tracking Dog Excellent tracking test. The TDX track is three to five hours old when the dog begins and is 800 to 1,000 yards long with five to seven changes of direction as well as cross-tracks by other people.

The Variable Surface Tracking title is designed to test a dog's real-world tracking skills in urban and wilderness settings. To earn the VST, a dog must follow a three- to five-hour-old track that may take him down streets, through buildings and empty lots, or other realistic terrains where there may be lots of competing scents. Finally, the AKC will issue a Champion Tracking title (CT) to a dog who has earned all three tracking titles.

More Sports

There's so much a Golden can do!

Thanks to the Golden Retriever's multi-tasking skills, there is an entire world of canine sports and activities that awaits you.

Dock Jumping: A thrilling sport for the water-loving Golden, a dock-dog performs a long jump by leaping off a dock of specified proportions to retrieve a toy thrown by her handler. The length (or height) of the jump is measured from the edge of the dock. The Dockdog organization also offers titling.

Flyball: Furiously fast, this relay race consists of a box loaded with tennis balls that ejects a ball whenever a dog jumps against the release. Four hurdles, set at a height appropriate for the shortest canine on the team of four, precede the box. Each dog individually leaps across the hurdles, hits the release, catches the ball and repeats her path back to the handler. The North American Flyball Association awards titles and maintains statistics.

Backpacking: Backpacking provides an excellent conditioning activity that burns off canine energy while you enjoy a healthy hike. Dogs need properly fitted equipment to prevent discomfort and chafing as they carry water, snacks or their own food for overnight trips. Several organizations offer backpacking titles, including the Dog Scouts of America.

Freestyle: Frequently referred to as "dancing with your dog," the harmonious teamwork between owner and dog seen in this sport would dazzle Fred Astaire. Freestyle deftly blends music, dance and dog training into an enjoyable, crowd-pleasing presentation. Individual teams combine traditional obedience moves with leg kicks, swirls, bows and a variety of imaginative moves. The Canine Freestyle Federation and the World Canine Freestyle Organization award titles.

Carting, Sledding, Skijoring, Scootering: Different approaches to pulling sports than weight pull, each of the aforementioned activities utilize your Golden's pulling strength and are coupled with firm obedience. Carting offers the most likelihood for titling; the rest mainly provide your Golden Retriever with great exercise and fun.

SHOW DOGS

When you purchase your Golden puppy, you must make it clear to the breeder whether you want one just as a lovable companion and pet, or if you hope to purchase a Golden Retriever with show prospects. No reputable breeder will sell you a puppy and tell you that he will definitely be show quality because so much can change during the early months of a puppy's development. If you do plan to show, what you hopefully will have acquired is a puppy with show potential.

To the novice, exhibiting a Golden in the ring may look easy, but it takes a lot of hard work and devotion to win at a show such as the annual Westminster Kennel Club Dog Show in New York City, not to mention a fair amount of luck, too!

The first concept that the canine novice learns when watching a dog show is that each dog first competes against members of his own breed. Once the judge has selected the best dog in each breed (Best of Breed) the chosen dog will compete with other dogs in his group. Finally, the dogs chosen first in each group will compete for the Best In Show title.

The second concept you must understand is that the dogs are not actually compared against one another. The judge compares each dog against the breed standard, the written description of the ideal dog approved by the AKC. While some early breed standards were indeed based on specific dogs who were famous or popular, many dedicated enthusiasts say that a perfect specimen as described in the standard has never walked into a show ring, has never been bred and, to the woe of dog breeders around the globe, does not exist. Breeders attempt to get as close to this ideal as possible with every litter, but theoretically the "perfect" dog is so elusive that it is impossible. (Even if the perfect dog were born, breeders and judges probably would never agree that he was perfect!)

If you are interested in exploring the world of conformation, your best bet is to join your local breed club or the national (or parent) club, the Golden Retriever Club of America. These clubs often host regional and national specialties, shows only for Golden Retrievers, which can include conformation as well as obedience and field trials. Even if you have no intention of competing with your Golden Retriever, a specialty is like a festival for lovers of the breed who congregate to share their favorite topic: Golden

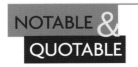

NOTABLE & QUOTABLE

With the Golden Retriever's natural retrieve drive, using a tossed toy as a reward can be exciting, motivating and a great way to teach sending commands in agility or obedience.

— Kathy Hoppe, a Golden owner and trainer from Presque Isle, Maine

Retrievers! Clubs also send out newsletters, and some organize training days and seminars providing owners the opportunity to learn more about their chosen breed. To locate the breed club closest to you, contact the AKC, which furnishes the rules and regulations for all of these events, plus general dog registration and other basic requirements of dog ownership.

CANINE GOOD CITIZEN

If obedience work sounds too regimented, but you'd still like your Golden Retriever to have a title, prepare him for the Canine Good Citizen test. This program is sponsored by the AKC, with tests administered by local dog clubs, private trainers and 4-H clubs.

To earn a CGC title, your Golden Retriever must be well-groomed and demonstrate the manners that all good dogs should exhibit. The CGC test requires a dog to follow the sit, lie down, stay and come cues, react appropriately to other dogs and distractions, allow a stranger to approach him, sit politely for petting, walk nicely on a loose leash, move through a crowd without going wild, calm down after play or praise and sit still for an examination by the judge. Rules are posted on the AKC's website.

THERAPY CHAMPS

Visiting nursing homes, hospices and hospitals with your Golden Retriever can be a tremendously satisfying experience. Many times, a dog can reach an individual who has otherwise withdrawn from the world. The people-oriented Golden can be a delightful therapy dog. This breed seems to have an affinity for children that makes them a natural for visiting children in hospitals or mental care facilities. Although a gentle disposition is definitely a plus, the often normally rambunctious dog seems to instinctively become gentler when introduced to those who are weak or ailing. Some basic obedience is, of course, a necessity for the therapy dog and a repertoire of tricks is a definite bonus. The sight of a clownish Golden Retriever "hamming it up" can help brighten most anyone's day.

Most facilities require a dog to have certification from a therapy dog organization. Therapy Dog International and the Delta Society are two such organizations. If your dog can pass a Canine Good Citizen test, earning certification will not be difficult. Certified therapy dog workers frequently get together a group and regularly make visitations in their area.

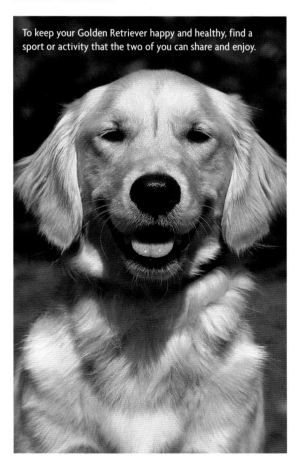

To keep your Golden Retriever happy and healthy, find a sport or activity that the two of you can share and enjoy.

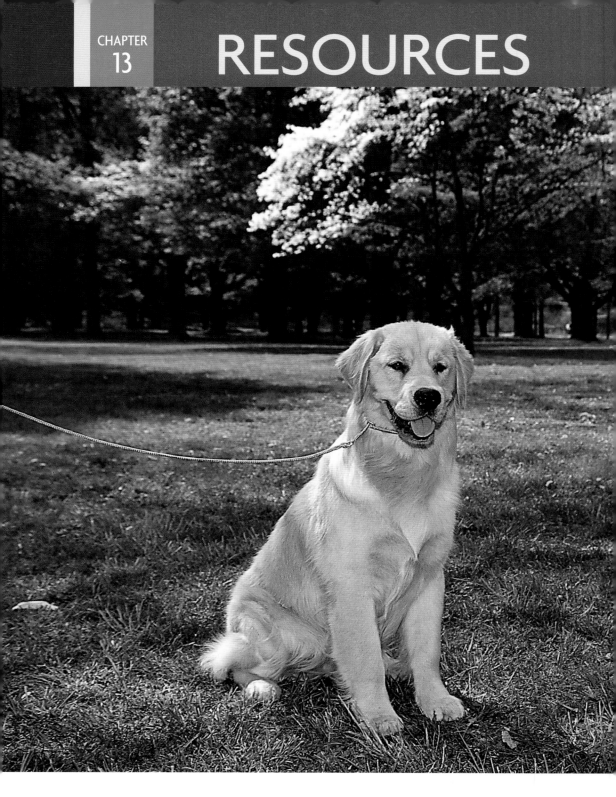

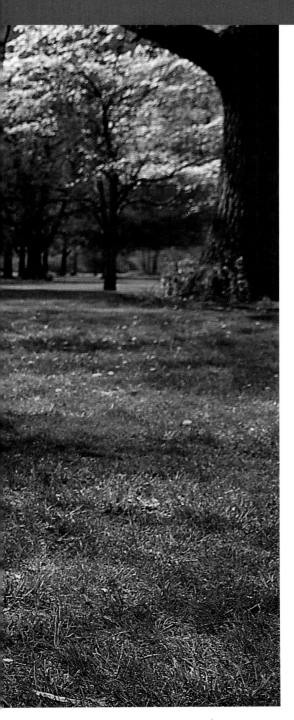

Smart owners can find out more information about this popular and fascinating breed by contacting the following organizations. They will be glad to help you dig deeper into the world of Golden Retrievers, and you won't even have to beg!

American Kennel Club: The AKC website offers information and links to conformation, tracking, rally, obedience and agility programs, member clubs and all things dog. www.akc.org

Canadian Kennel Club: Our northern neighbor's oldest kennel club is similar to the AKC in the states. www.ckc.ca

Canine Performance Events: Sports to keep dogs active. www.k9cpe.com

Dog Scouts of America: Take your dog to camp! www.dogscouts.com

Golden Retriever Club of America: This is the national parent breed club of the American Kennel Club. www.grca.org

Love on a Leash: Your Golden has a lot of love to give! www.loveonaleash.org

National Association of Professional Pet Sitters: Hire someone to watch your dog when you leave town. www.petssitters.org

it's a **Fact**

The **American Kennel Club** was established in 1884. It is America's oldest kennel club. The **United Kennel Club** is the second oldest in the United States and began registering dogs in 1898.

North American Dog Agility Council: This site provides links to clubs, obedience trainers and agility trainers in the United States and Canada. www.nadac.com

The North American Hunting Retriever Association: Get involved in the sport your dog was created for. www.nahranews.org

Therapy Dogs Inc.: Get your Golden involved in therapy. www.therapydogs.com

Therapy Dogs International: Find more therapy dog info here: www.tdi-dog.org

United Kennel Club: The UKC offers several events offered by the AKC, including agility, conformation and obedience. In addition, the UKC offers competitions in hunting and dog sport (companion and protective events). Both the UKC and the AKC offer programs for junior handlers, ages 2 to 18. www.ukcdogs.com

United States Dog Agility Association: The USDAA has information on training, clubs and events in the United States, Canada, Mexico and overseas. www.usdaa.com

World Canine Freestyle Organization: Dancing with your dog is fun! www.world caninefreestyle.org

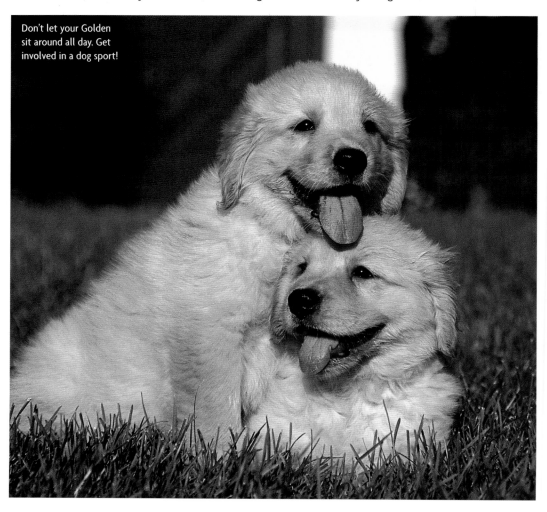

Don't let your Golden sit around all day. Get involved in a dog sport!

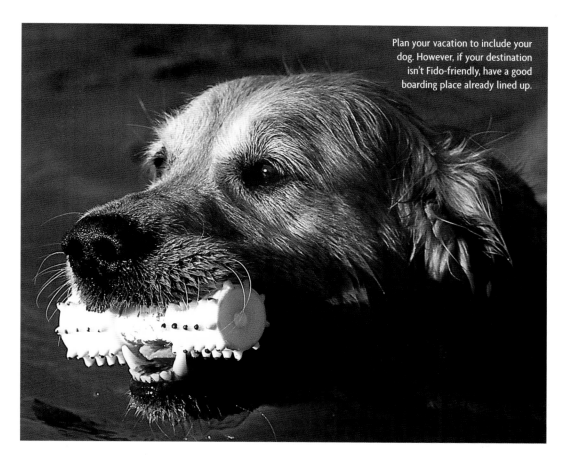

Plan your vacation to include your dog. However, if your destination isn't Fido-friendly, have a good boarding place already lined up.

BOARDING

So you want to take a family vacation — and you want to include all members of the family. You usually make arrangements for accommodations ahead of time anyway, but this is imperative when traveling with a dog. You do not want to make an overnight stop at the only place around for miles only to discover that the hotel doesn't allow dogs. You also don't want to reserve a room for your family without confirming that you are traveling with a Golden because if it is against the hotel's policy, you may not have a place to stay.

Alternatively, if you are traveling and choose not to bring your Golden, you will have to make arrangements for him. Some options are to leave him with a reliable family member or a neighbor, or have a trusted friend stop by often or stay at your house. Another option is leaving your Golden at a reputable boarding kennel.

If you choose to board him at a kennel, visit in advance to see the facilities and check how clean they are, and where the dogs are kept. Talk to some of the employees and see how they treat the dogs. Do they spend time with the dogs either during play or exercise? Also, find out the kennel's policy on required vaccinations. This is for all of the dogs' safety because when dogs are kept together, there is a greater risk of diseases being passed between them.

HOME STAFFING

For the Golden Retriever parent who works all day, a pet sitter or dog walker may be the perfect solution for your lonely retriever longing for a midday stroll. Smart dog owners should approach local high schools or community centers if they don't have a neighbor who is interested in a part-time commitment. When you interview potential dog walkers, consider their experience with dogs, as well as your Golden's rapport with the candidate. (Golden Retrievers are excellent judges of character.) You should always check references before entrusting your dog and opening your home to a new dog walker.

For an owner's long-term absence, such as a business trip or vacation, many Golden Retriever owners welcome the services of a pet sitter. It's usually less stressful on the dog to stay home with a pet sitter than to be boarded in a kennel. Pet sitters also may be more affordable than a week's stay at a full-service doggie day care.

Pet sitters must be even more reliable than dog walkers because the dog is depending on his surrogate owner for all of his needs over an extended period. Owners are advised to hire a certified pet sitter through the National Association of Professional Pet Sitters (www.petsitters.org). NAPPS provides online and toll-free pet

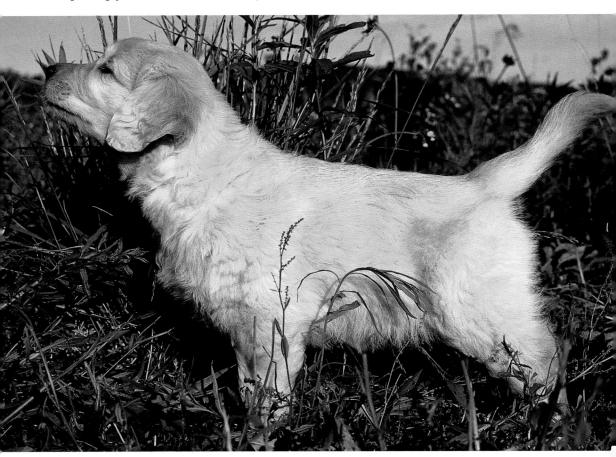

sitter locator services. The nonprofit organization only certifies serious-minded, professional individuals who are knowledgeable in canine behavior, nutrition, health and safety. Whether or not you take your Golden with you, always keep your Golden Retriever's best interest at heart when planning a trip.

SCHOOL'S IN SESSION

Puppy kindergarten, which is usually open to dogs between 3 to 6 months of age, allows puppies to learn and socialize with other dogs and people in a structured setting. Classes helps to socialize your Golden Retriever so that he will enjoy going places with you and be a well-behaved member in public gatherings. They prepare him for adult obedience classes and for a lifetime of social experiences he will have with your friends and his furry friends. The problem with most puppy kindergarten classes is that they only occur one night a week.

If you're home during the day, you may be able to find places to take your puppy so he can socialize. Just be careful about dog parks and other places that are open to any dog. An experience with a dog bully can undo all the good your training classes have done.

If you work, your puppy may be home alone all day, a tough situation for a Golden Retriever. Chances are he can't hold himself that long, so your potty training will be undermined — unless you're teaching him to use an indoor potty. Also, by the time you come home, he'll be bursting with energy, and you may think that he's hyperactive and uncontrollable.

The only suitable answer for the working professional with a Golden Retriever is doggie day care. Most large cities have some sort of day care, whether it's a boarding kennel that keeps your dog in a run or a full-service day care that offers training, play time and even spa facilities. They range from a person who keeps a few dogs at his or her home to a state-of-the-art facility built just for dogs. Many of the more sophisticated doggie day cares offer webcams so you can see what your dog is up to throughout the day. Things to look for:

- escape-proof facilities, such as gates in doorways that lead outside
- inoculation requirements for new dogs
- midday meals for young dogs
- obedience training (if offered), using reward-based methods
- safe and comfortable nap areas
- screening of dogs for aggression
- small groups of similar sizes and ages
- toys and playground equipment, such as tunnels and chutes
- trained staff, with an adequate number to supervise the dogs (no more than 10 to 15 dogs per person)
- a webcam

Remember to keep your dog's leash slack when interacting with other dogs. It is not unusual for a dog to pick out one or two canine neighbors to dislike. If you know there's bad blood, step off to the side and find a barrier, such as a parked car, between the dogs. If there are no barriers to be had, move to the side of the walkway, cue your Golden to sit, stay and watch you until her nemesis passes; then continue your walk.

SMART TIP!

CAR TRAVEL

You should try to acclimate your Golden Retriever to riding in a car at an early age. You may or may not take him in the car often, but at the very least he will need to go to the vet once in a while, and you do not want these trips to be traumatic for your dog or troublesome for you. The safest way for your dog to ride in the car is in his crate. If he uses a crate in the house, you can use the same crate for travel.

Another option is a specially made safety harness for dogs, which straps your Golden in the car much like a seat belt would. Do not let the dog roam loose in the vehicle; this is very dangerous! If you should make

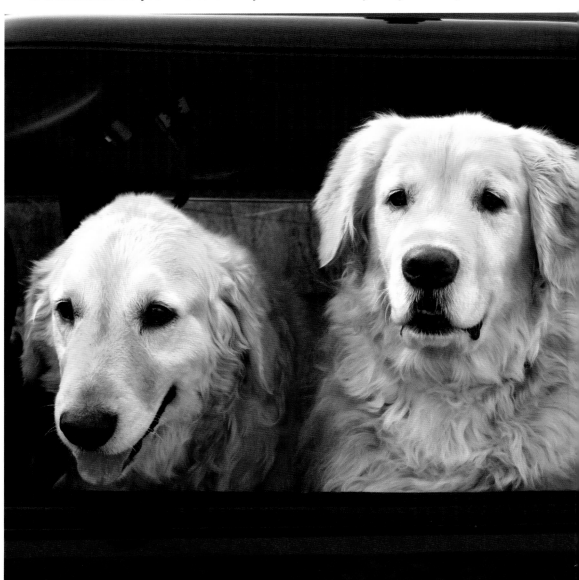

an abrupt stop, your dog can be thrown and injured. If your dog starts climbing on you while you are driving, you will not be able to concentrate on the road. It is an unsafe situation for everyone — human and canine.

For long trips, stop often to let your Golden relieve himself. Take along whatever you need to clean up after him, including paper towels should he have an accident in the car or suffer from motion sickness.

IDENTIFICATION

Your Golden is your valued companion and friend. That is why you always keep a close eye on him, and you have made sure that he cannot escape from the yard or wriggle out of his collar and run away from you. However, accidents can happen and there may come a time when your Golden Retriever unexpectedly gets separated from you. If this should occur, the first thing on your mind will be finding him. Proper identification, including an ID tag, a tattoo and possibly a microchip, will increase the chances of his being returned to you safely and quickly.

An ID tag on a collar or harness is the primary means of identifying a lost pet (and ID licenses are required in many cities). Although inexpensive and easy to read, collars and ID tags can come off or be taken off.

A microchip doesn't get lost. The microchip is embedded underneath the dog's skin and contains a unique ID number that is read by scanners. It comes in handy for identifying lost or stolen pets. However, to be effective, the microchip must be registered in a national database. Smart owners will register their dog and regularly check that their contact information is kept up-to-date.

However, one thing to keep in mind is that not every shelter or veterinary clinic has a scanner, nor do most folks who might pick up and try to return a lost pet. Your best best? Get both!

Did You Know?

Some communities have created regular dog runs and separate spaces for small dogs. These small-dog runs are ideal for introducing puppies to the dog park experience. The runs are smaller, the participants are smaller and their owners are often more vigilant because they are used to watching out for their fragile companions.

INDEX

INDEX

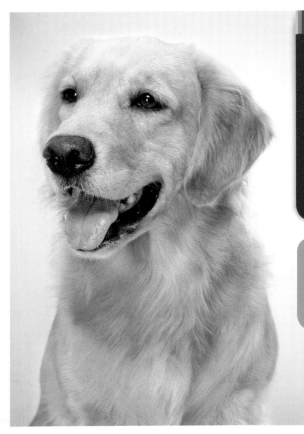
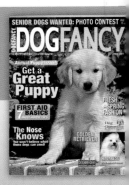
GOLDEN RETRIEVER, a Smart Owner's Guide™
part of the Kennel Club Books® Interactive Series™

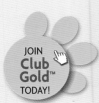

JOIN
Club
Gold™
TODAY!

LIBRARY OF CONGRESS CATALOGING-IN-PUBLICATION DATA

Golden retriever : a smart owner's guide / from the editors of Dog fancy magazine.
   p. cm. — (Kennel Club Books interactive series)
Includes bibliographical references and index.
ISBN 978-1-59378-763-9
1. Golden retriever. I. Dog fancy (San Juan Capistrano, Calif.)
SF429.G63G545 2010
636.752'7—dc22

                   2009040985